A LIVING
HOPE

*EXAMINING HISTORY'S MOST IMPORTANT EVENT
AND WHAT IT MEANS FOR THE WORLD*

MATT HODGES

LUCIDBOOKS

A Living Hope: Examining History's Most Important Event and What it Means for the World

Copyright © 2017 Matt Hodges
Published by Lucid Books in Houston, TX.
www.LucidBooksPublishing.com

All rights reserved. No part of this publication may be reproduced, stored in a retrieval system, or transmitted in any form by any means, electronic, mechanical, photocopy, recording, or otherwise, without the prior permission of the publisher, except as provided for by USA copyright law.

Unless otherwise noted, Scripture quotations are from the ESV® Bible (The Holy Bible, English Standard Version®), copyright © 2001 by Crossway, a publishing ministry of Good News Publishers. Used by permission. All rights reserved.

ISBN-10: 163296144X
ISBN-13: 9781632961440
eISBN-10: 1632961458
eISBN-13: 9781632961457

Special Sales: Most Lucid Books titles are available in special quantity discounts. Custom imprinting or excerpting can also be done to fit special needs. Contact Lucid Books at www.lucidbookspublishing.com.

To Bapa
Who taught me not only how to learn
But also how to love doing so

Table of Contents

Introduction..1

PART I: THE FRAMEWORK
Chapter 1: The Objectivity of Religious Claims....................7
Chapter 2: The Centrality of the Resurrection....................19
Chapter 3: Considering Atheism..27
Chapter 4: Considering Agnosticism..................................51

PART II: THE EVIDENCE
Chapter 5: The Historical Documents................................63
Chapter 6: The Resurrection Accounts...............................83
Chapter 7: A Life-Changing Event.....................................91
Chapter 8: Alternative Theories.......................................101

PART III: THE INVITATION
Chapter 9: From Head to Heart......................................119
Chapter 10: A Living Hope..143
Conclusion..157

Acknowledgments...165
Additional Resources..167
Notes..169

Introduction

Christianity, if false, is of no importance, and if true, of infinite importance. The only thing it cannot be is moderately important.

—C. S. Lewis

In an Easter sermon, Tim Keller, a minister in New York City once shared an illustration that has always stuck with me. To paraphrase, he said that if you received a letter on a law firm's letterhead telling you that a distant relative whom you never knew left you millions of dollars in his will, you'd be skeptical. You'd be correct to question its validity and not blindly give away all your information in response. However, you also wouldn't throw it away without at least looking into it. At first, you may think it's too good to be true, but you wouldn't toss it in the garbage until you were sure. The offer is simply too amazing—too life-changing—to dismiss without consideration and investigation.

He then likened that anecdote to the resurrection of Jesus, making the point that the offer of Christianity is likewise too amazing—*more* amazing, even, than a monetary fortune—to dismiss without serious consideration and investigation. Of course, like the person who received the mysterious inheritance, we're likely skeptical that an offer this generous—this outrageous—has any validity. If it sounds too good to be true, it usually is, right? But if there's even a chance the offer is genuine, is it not worth serious consideration? That consideration—that investigation of the offer—is the purpose of this book.

If the claim of the Christian worldview is false, then it doesn't matter at all. But if it is true, then it matters more than anything. In other words, if Jesus of Nazareth really was a historical man who lived, died, and, most importantly, came back from the dead, then that truth stands above all other truth. It shapes everything we know about the world. It's not merely one religious claim among many; it's a reality-defining, paradigm-altering story. If Jesus really resurrected, it changes everything. I've wrestled with the evidence and the implications, and I'm convinced that Jesus came back from the dead. I believe this world-changing event *did* occur. And my hope is to persuade others to believe the same.

Understandably, when terms such as *religion* and *persuasion* are blended, it can cause us to put our guard up. Should we not let people simply believe what they believe? To each his own, right? In actuality, though, to believe such an event occurred (and therefore to believe in all of its implications) and to not try to persuade others to believe the same is far less considerate than keeping it to yourself. The significance of the Easter message is too great to treat as personal religion.

If Jesus Really Resurrected, It Changes Everything

Throughout his ministry, the apostle Paul, who wrote most of the New Testament, often sought to persuade an audience regarding Jesus's true identity and purpose. Some translations say that he sought to reason with or convince them.

Paul went into the synagogue, and on three Sabbath days he **reasoned with them** *from the Scriptures.*

And some of them were **persuaded** *and joined Paul and Silas.*

Paul entered the synagogue and spoke boldly there for three months, **arguing persuasively** *about the kingdom of God* (emphasis added).[1]

He did this despite the fact that many of the people he engaged with disagreed with him. They came from different backgrounds, were raised in different traditions, and held different convictions about the world. Yet he engaged them because he understood the significance of what he was communicating. What's more, the people he engaged chose to listen and allowed him to argue his case. Why? Because they understood if there is even the slightest chance that he was right about Jesus, it would be incumbent on them to listen. Such news would be far too significant to wave aside without serious consideration. So if Paul was going to speak to them about it, they understood the value of lending their ears.

With that said, here is what I would like to ask of you. Take this book one chapter at a time. If, at the very least, your curiosity is piqued enough to read the first chapter, do just that. If by the end of that chapter you're willing to consider the next point, just read one more chapter (and yes, I'm keenly aware that I'm not revolutionizing book reading by suggesting that you read the chapters in succession). What I mean is that sometimes discussions of religion get muddied, and each individual consideration is not treated on its own, as it should be.

Whether you read this book as a long-time Christian, an open-minded seeker, a hardened skeptic, or a person who accepted the truth of Christianity just yesterday, my hope is that the historical, objective, unwavering truth of Jesus's resurrection will be evident, and with it will come peace, comfort, and assurance in a world that otherwise provides little of any.

PART I
THE FRAMEWORK

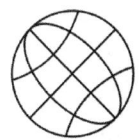

Chapter 1
The Objectivity of Religious Claims

If you sincerely believe a lie, you will suffer the consequences. You must not only be sincere, but you must be right.
—*Charles Spurgeon*

Imagine if you asked someone, "What is two plus two?" and he or she responded, "Well, it's tough to really *know* what two plus two is, isn't it? Isn't that what we're all trying to figure out? I think what's important is that we all believe for ourselves what we get when we add two and two together. If those beliefs in those particular answers help us become better people, then I'm all for whatever answers people give." Or, what if you asked someone, "Who was the third president of the United States?" and they replied, "Well, I was raised to believe that John F. Kennedy was the third president, and that belief was central to my identity growing up. I'm very grateful for it. I think it's valid and it helps a great many people. However, as I matured, I came to discover for myself that it was, in fact, Theodore Roosevelt. Now, it brings me peace in hard times to know that Theodore Roosevelt was the third president, but I certainly think someone can believe John F. Kennedy or anyone else was the third president as well if that brings that person the same peace that I've found in my truth."

It's clear that neither of the above is an acceptable answer. The questions are seeking objective, concrete answers. Personal opinions and inner peace have no effect on the addition of two quantities or the order of the presidents. Objectively, arithmetic is accomplished independently of feelings, and events in space-time occur with no regard to whether or not they bring us comfort. If either question were posed in a classroom, a student would not be praised as open-minded or progressive for offering either of the above answers. The teacher would simply say, "Sorry, that's incorrect." Why can the teacher tell the student he or she is wrong without fear of getting fired? Because truth is objective. It's measurable. And in those scenarios, it's the teacher's job to inform the student what that objective truth is.

Every truth claim, by definition, is either right or wrong. Just as we hope classroom teachers would agree with us, we know that truth cannot be relative. There is an objectively true answer to every question. Of course, the answer very well may be, "We cannot answer that question" or "We cannot know the answer to that question." But the unanswerableness of the question is, then, either true or false itself. To the question "What is two plus two?" we can answer "four." That answer is true. To the question, "What was Abraham Lincoln's favorite color?" we could offer the answer "blue." Perhaps that answer is based on evidence found in a diary or in a recorded conversation with someone who knew him very well. But what if there is no evidence for that answer? What if no record exists about his favorite color? We could then say, "We don't know" or "We can't know based on the information we have." Presumably, our answer in that case is still correct.

It is this distinction between answerable and unanswerable questions that frames everything that follows in this book. Too often, we approach questions such as "From where did the universe come?" or "What happens after we die?" or "Is there a God and what is he like?" as if their answers are dependent on personal opinions and experience. They're relegated to the "unanswerable" category, and then given answers that are founded on emotions or presumptions, oftentimes unsubstantiated ones. To be sure, I'm not claiming that answers to questions of the universe's origin or the existence and nature of God are as simple as our "two plus two" example. But we ought to be aware of the tendency to give such questions a "subjective" or "unanswerable" classification, particularly without first examining all the options and evidence.

Let's take the afterlife, for example. Everyone at one point or another has likely pondered, "What happens when we die?" As sensitive as the subject may be, the truth is that there *is* an objective reality about what happens after death. Someone believing that one thing happens while someone else believing that another thing happens does not make both people correct. If person A believes in reincarnation, while person B believes there is no existence after death at all, both people, while entitled to their own beliefs, cannot be right. The same reality that person A faces after death *will* face person B as well, whether one of them or neither of them believes it. The same principle is true for the origin of the universe or the existence of God. Again, person A may believe that God's nature is X, while person B could believe his nature is Y or even that God doesn't exist at all. Each belief can be held sincerely, but neither belief has any bearing on the fundamental reality. Either one person is correct or neither is correct. Both can believe as they wish, but both cannot be affirmed simultaneously as correct.

With issues such as these, it is fair to call the knowability of the answer into question; we cannot, however, call the objectivity of the answer into question. Just because the answer to a question may be difficult to discern doesn't mean the answer can be whatever we want it to be. An answer may be elusive, but that does not mean that it's relative. There is one true reality for all such matters: life after death, the existence of God (and subsequently his nature, character, and interaction with the world), the origin of the universe, the nature of humankind, and so on). All these are topics that have objectively truthful answers, completely independent of what person A or person B or anyone else believes about them. All worldviews, whether religious or otherwise, should be founded on knowable, objective evidence. Only by taking this approach will we be able to discover which worldview is actually true.

Even that idea—discerning which worldview is "true"—offends many people. Oftentimes, statements of this nature are met with rebuttals such as "It's arrogant to claim to know the truth" or "It's closed-minded to think one religion is true and others are not." And if our worldviews are merely a matter of blind faith and sincere

> *Just because the answer to a question may be difficult to discern doesn't mean the answer can be whatever we want it to be.*

The Objectivity of Religious Claims

belief, then I would agree entirely, and a statement about a true worldview could very well be deemed offensive. However, since our worldview should be determined by the same deductive process and reasonable thinking we use to answer questions of arithmetic and historical fact, then the claim of a true worldview, at its core, is not an affront on or insult to other faiths. It is rather simply an examination of evidence and the conclusions drawn from that evidence.

The truth is, we all believe something about the world. We all subscribe to a worldview that we believe to be true, and that worldview is based on information that we believe to be true. Even the belief that all worldviews are true is itself a worldview—a worldview that someone can believe to be true or not. That means that even the belief that there is no objective truth is itself an objective truth claim. If someone says "I believe that all truth is relative; no worldview is objectively true," it would be perfectly fair to reply, "Even the worldview that you hold? Is your truth—that all truth is relative—also relative?" In such a case, the foundational, objectively true belief on which this person bases his or her existence is that nothing is objectively true. The irony is apparent.

All of that is to say that every worldview is founded on truth claims. If the truth claims of a worldview are false, then why operate according to that worldview? However, if they are true, then why live according to anything *but* that worldview? The important task is, of course, to determine which truth claims are actually true and which are not. No one is about to deem someone else closed-minded or intolerant for claiming that two plus two equals four. Why? Because it is an objectively true statement. The statement is based on a reality that cares nothing about one's belief, however sincere it may be, that two plus two is, in fact, five.

Religious Claims Are Truth Claims

Consider the following scenario. You encounter a man poised on the edge of a tall building. He's standing ten stories up, he's wearing cardboard wings, and he's about to jump off. From the ground level, you shout, "Don't jump! If you jump, you will fall!" The man replies, "Ha! How closed-minded of you! Perhaps *your* worldview is one in which I am subject to gravity, but in my heart of hearts, I know with certainty that I can leap off this edge and take flight!" Does that settle it? Should you feel guilty for claiming a worldview in which gravity isn't something we can *choose* whether or not we're subject to a worldview in which that which goes up must, in fact, come down? If he is entitled to his own worldview—his own perception of reality—then would it be arrogant to insist that despite his most sincere beliefs, he will be subject to gravity just like everyone else? Certainly not. We know that the man's distaste for the "universal" in Newton's law of universal gravitation has no bearing on its truthfulness. The universal effect of gravity is either true or not true, independent of whether a person believes it.

Although admittedly farfetched, this analogy is a useful parallel to our discussion. The man who is about to jump is betting on something—just like we do with our beliefs about the world. He's betting on the fact that his *belief* about the world—the *belief* that gravity is something he can choose to defy—is true. And when he is faced with the plea not to jump, he has two options: (1) dismiss the

The Objectivity of Religious Claims

opposing worldview because it is contrary to his own and, frankly, rather offensive (after all, who is this person on the ground claiming authority on whether he will fall or not?), or (2) consider his inability to escape the effect of gravity and thoroughly investigate it before staking so much on his current beliefs. Of course, we'd hope that option two is the clear choice, because what ultimately matters is not if a worldview is firmly and sincerely *believed* but whether or not it is *correct*. Believing that he can defy gravity does not guarantee his safety. He must actually be able to do so in order to be safe. There is a disconnect between his beliefs and reality, and that disconnect ought to be addressed and remedied.

On the other hand, the person who encounters this man and recognizes that disconnect and, more importantly, the potential ramifications of that disconnect, now has an obligation to (1) plead with him to reconsider his beliefs and (2) explain what he should believe instead and why. The same is true when discussing matters of faith and religion. Our religious beliefs are simply a way of saying, "I believe this to be true about the world." Underneath the rituals and worship services and holiday traditions lies a fundamental belief about our reality. And since these truth claims are aimed at answering life's most important questions, they should be the beliefs that we both scrutinize the most and champion the loudest. Like our gravity illustration, if you sincerely believe something to be true and believe that someone else's denial of that truth has serious implications, then it's your obligation to do your best to inform that person of the truth.

Real Tolerance

"But, isn't it intolerant to tell someone that his or her religious views are wrong?" This is a common objection raised when discussing matters of faith and religion. Some say, "Who are we to say that this religion or that faith is right or wrong? Everyone should be able to believe whatever he or she wants, and it's not our place to judge or correct." By that logic, though, who are we to tell the man on the edge of the building that he will fall if he jumps? Shouldn't he be allowed to believe whatever he wishes? Is it not, then, intolerant to tell him he will fall?

Here's where understanding the true definition of tolerance becomes essential. Tolerance is not the acceptance of all ideas and beliefs as valid and right. Tolerance is accepting all people as valuable despite the fact that you believe their ideas or beliefs are incorrect. Obviously, people can be wrong about things. What's more, if all beliefs were true and valid, then there would be nothing to tolerate.

Tolerance is not the acceptance of all ideas and beliefs as valid and right. Tolerance is accepting all people as valuable despite the fact that you believe their ideas or beliefs are incorrect.

So the moment you see the man about to jump, you are able to tell him he is wrong about his ability to defy gravity, and in doing so, you are actually treating him as valuable. You care enough about his fate to disagree with his beliefs, challenge his beliefs, and ultimately, possibly change his beliefs. You do so because gravity is a universal truth, and to believe otherwise is to not only be incorrect, but also to be in danger.

If someone is convinced that his or her religious worldview is true, then one of the most inconsiderate things he or she can do is to not try to convince others of it. If you sincerely believe something about the world that could have consequences for people, it's not tolerant—it's not loving—to avoid attempts to change their worldview. Knowing that two sets of opposing beliefs cannot both be objectively true and still treating them as if they can be is not tolerant—it's irresponsible. This means that someone who believes that the Christian worldview (or any other worldview, for that matter) is objectively true has the obligation to not only acknowledge that others can be wrong in their beliefs, but also to seek to convince them of its truthfulness. It's not a matter of persuading someone merely toward an inner peace but toward a belief that's as concrete as two plus two equals four.

A Reasonable Faith

There is a lot of confusion surrounding the true nature of Christianity—or what it is at the core. Oftentimes, it's thought of as a particular set of ethical teachings, perhaps necessary for either achieving a more fulfilling life or for earning favor with God. Other times, it's viewed as a source of personal comfort and peace. For others, it's regarded as a cultural or familial identity, tied more closely to our heritage and geography than to our beliefs about the world. But these are not, in and of themselves, Christianity.

The Christian worldview isn't centered on certain moral teachings or cultural identifiers; it's centered on a story—the story of how our world will be renewed and restored to perfection through one man, Jesus. We'll get to what that means more fully later on. But it's essential that we begin with that framework because there are many superfluous debates that surround the topic of Christianity that can be largely unhelpful in the process of examining its truthfulness and validity. My hope is to catalyze a serious consideration and discussion of the true worldview of Christianity, not the claims represented by social media, figureheads, or that one relative who wants to discuss only religion and politics at Thanksgiving. This book is not simply about evaluating one religion among many; it's about evaluating truth claims.

Because the central claim of the Christian worldview is concrete and not abstract, it is unique among religious claims. Often, faith and reason are pitted against each other. People assume that you can either live a life based on fact or on faith. Christianity, though, is a marriage of the two—of the heart and the head. It's belief, yes, but it's belief in facts. Believing in Jesus is believing in the objective accomplishments of a real historical figure, not merely appreciating his teachings and example. The Christian worldview is based on evidence; it isn't blind faith. In fact, according to the first Christians, it's anything but blind faith. We read in John's Gospel:

> *Then Simon Peter came, following him, and went into the tomb. He saw the linen cloths lying there, and the face cloth, which had been on Jesus' head, not lying with the linen cloths but folded up in a place by itself. Then the other disciple, who had reached the tomb first, also went in, and* **he saw and believed.**[2]

Notice the order: "he saw and believed." This disciple,

The Objectivity of Religious Claims

John, had his beliefs—his worldview—changed by what he saw. He had new evidence, and it was in what he saw to be true that he found the source for what he was going to believe. His belief—his faith—wasn't blind at all. It was the very opposite. He used his eyes, and he reasoned from what his eyes could see. That is what sets Christianity apart from all other worldviews. It's not merely a religion. It's not merely a tradition. And it's not merely faith. It is all of those things in one way or another, but its foundation is built on its historical, objective truthfulness.

C. S. Lewis argued that people should not accept Christianity because it's relevant or exciting or personally satisfying; rather, they should only accept it because it's true. And only when you accept its truthfulness, he says, will you then be able to find it relevant, exciting, and personally satisfying. The other feelings, emotions, and benefits that the Christian worldview provides are only going to be experienced, at least with any lasting assurance, if the worldview itself is actually true. Otherwise, the emotional benefits will waver along with all of life's circumstances. If our beliefs are tied to our circumstances, then when our circumstances fail us, so will our beliefs. That is why it's essential that we base our beliefs about the world on facts. If something is provable—if we can find assurance in it independent of extenuating factors—then we can have true faith in it no matter what else may come our way. The next step, then, is to argue why Christianity is a verifiable truth and not simply one religion

If our beliefs are tied to our circumstances, then when our circumstances fail us, so will our beliefs.

or philosophy among many. To do so, we must define its central claim and show why it must remain central.

Chapter 2
The Centrality of the Resurrection

And if Christ has not been raised, then our preaching is in vain and your faith is in vain.

—*The Apostle Paul*

The Philosophical Centrality of the Resurrection

As we argued in the previous chapter, worldview claims are objective statements. It's a statement of belief regarding the world we live in—how it was created, what its purpose is, who we are as those who inhabit it, and so forth. And, again, that means that any such claim can be right or it can be wrong. Either our beliefs about the world and our origin and existence are true, or they aren't. It follows, then, that we should seek to have our beliefs rooted in reliable evidence. If we're going to claim something about the reality we inhabit, there ought to be a concrete reason for why we believe that reality is, in fact, real.

For those that hold to the Christian worldview, the resurrection of Jesus is that concrete reason. If such an event actually occurred in history—if a man literally rose from the dead—then it changes everything for us. It would be truly a reality-defining event. It would shape (or at least *should* shape) how we think about and approach every aspect of our existence. On the other hand, if it did not happen, then the Christian worldview would be at best one religious choice among many, and at worst a giant hoax. If there exists no objective evidence to validate a worldview, Christian or otherwise, then anyone's guess is as good as the next person's. A worldview is only as good as the evidence upon which it is based.

> *A worldview is only as good as the evidence upon which it is based.*

The Christian worldview is based on the identity and accomplishments of Jesus. If he was who he says he was, then everything in our world is shaped by that truth. Examining the historical validity of his resurrection is the means of determining just that. Was Jesus merely another man who began a movement and happened to get lucky with the results, or was he far more?

Jesus's Divinity

What kind of person makes the claim that he is God incarnate and can come back from the dead, as Jesus did many times? C. S. Lewis wrote in his book *Mere Christianity* that such a person is either a liar or a lunatic. In other words, a man who says he can supernaturally transcend the laws of nature is either intentionally deceiving people or is himself deceived. That is, of course, unless he *can* actually come back from the dead. This is what refers to as a trilemma, or dilemma that has three instead of two alternatives. With Jesus, we must choose (1) if he was intentionally trying to gain followers by lying to them, (2) if he was delusional and believed himself to be divine, or (3) if he was truly who he claimed to be—God in the flesh. The choice depends on one simple fact: whether or not he literally and physically came back from the dead. That is why Jesus's resurrection is the foundational claim of Christianity. If Jesus really did rise from the dead, then it's safe to say that we have no grounds on which we can refute his divinity.

Few things, if any, can substantiate a claim of divinity as effectively as a resurrection. Think about it. How could someone ever argue with a man who died and then, some days later, was alive again? Would it not be clear that we are dealing with someone much more powerful and capable than we are? If we knew of a man with that kind of power, we would be obligated to place him in a different category than our own. We could not say, "Sure, he can bend the laws of nature to his will, but are we sure he's not just like us?"

Let's consider James, the brother of Jesus. We know that for most of his life James was not convinced that his brother was divine.[3] He was, like many were and many are, skeptical of the claims of Jesus. And, truthfully, who can blame him? Imagine if your brother or a close relative tried to convince you that he was actually a divine being. You would be wary, and rightly so. But then, all of a sudden James changed his tune. Something happened, and James became an avid supporter of his brother's teachings and claims of divine authority. He even became one of the foremost leaders in the early days of the church. What happened? No matter how skeptical he was, no matter how certain he was that his brother was either crazy or deceptive, he could not argue with what he saw—he saw his brother actually die, get buried, and come back from the dead. Of course, that was proof enough for him of Jesus's divinity, as it should be proof enough for anyone.

That is why Jesus's resurrection is so important, because no matter how skeptical we may be of the claims of Jesus, if he did, in fact, come back from the dead, how can we refute them? How can we doubt him? The power to bring oneself back from the dead proves that there is a supernatural ability far above our own. And if Jesus proved himself divine, what rationality can we throw at him? If he did come back from the dead, we must admit our limitations; namely, that we cannot do as he did and therefore cannot claim the authority he claims. There is no debating with someone who can reverse death itself. Few would be foolish enough to argue like this: "Yes, I see that you alone are free from the confines of the natural world as we know it, but have you considered *my* point of view?"

The apostle Paul, when writing to the church at Corinth, makes clear how much hinges on whether or not Jesus came back from the dead. Essentially, he argues that if Jesus is still in the grave, then why would he preach to them at all? Why would he teach about him? And, most importantly, why would he tell them to trust him with their lives? If he was just another man, then he's just one more option among many to consider for a source of teachings. If he did, however, come back from the dead—if he's more than just a man—how could they trust their lives to anyone else? Who else would they rather follow? Who could they trust with matters of life, purpose, death, and the afterlife than he who stands above it all?

Whom do we trust?

Ultimately, that is what it all comes down to: whom are we going to trust with decisions that impact our lives and eternities? We're all going to trust someone, be it ourselves or someone else, and there are many options from which we can choose, so we must choose carefully. That means we must be clear on the criteria we deem worthy of consideration in making that choice. If we are going to entrust our lives and eternity to someone, how do we make that decision? What factors are we going to consider? It is hard to imagine enough merits in favor of ourselves that can effectively outweigh the merits of Jesus, who can say, "I am divine. I have existed since the beginning of time. I have the entire universe under my authority. And I proved it all by coming back from the dead." How can we respond to that? There is no GPA, no degree, no job, no skill set, no life experience whatsoever that can measure up to that. There is no résumé we can conjure up that gives us more credibility than someone who can say to death itself, "No."

Historical Centrality of the Resurrection

The early Christians agreed with the premise that Jesus's resurrection earned him the right to claim authority and to be given allegiance. They understood the importance of the resurrection and its implications. In fact, their confidence regarding the afterlife, because of what Jesus accomplished, was their most notable characteristic. We'll come back to this later, but it's worth mentioning that even those who had disdain for the early church could not doubt their incredible confidence when confronted with persecution. Galen, a physician and prominent critic of the early church, noted this about followers of Jesus: "Now we see the people called Christians drawing their faith from parables [and miracles], and yet sometimes acting in the same way [as those who philosophize]. For their contempt of death [and of its sequel] is patent to us every day."[4]

"Their contempt of death and of its sequel" is one of the most notable marks of the Christian, he said. Essentially, he is observing that Christians were not afraid of death and what lies beyond, like everyone else. They disrespected death itself, the great enemy of us all. They were not shaken or intimidated by its threat—a threat that many of them had to deal with often.

Counting the cost

In the church's earliest stages, the Christian worldview did not bring with it the peace of mind and social comforts that many Christians enjoy today. Many of us today, Christian or otherwise, enjoy the freedom of religion afforded to us by our government, but the same cannot be said for Christians in the first century. If they were going to claim the Christian worldview, they were going to need a tangible, unwavering reason to do so. When faced with threats of being ostracized, tortured, and even executed, they had to cling to something that was true—not just true for them, but objectively, certainly true. They needed a real hope.

Ask yourself this: What kind of promise would it take for me to be willing to give up everything? My livelihood? My reputation? My possessions? My own life? It would have to be both undoubtedly true and unimaginably beneficial. Something can be true and still not be worth sacrificing everything for. It's a true statement that combining red and blue makes purple, but that's hardly the kind of statement to which you would give your entire life and identity. It's true, but it does not provide substance and hope for your life. Likewise, something could potentially be incredibly beneficial and still not be certain enough to give your whole self to. The claim "if you buy a lottery ticket, you could win a fortune" is true, but it would not be advisable to sacrifice all of your time and resources to gathering lottery tickets. If something is worth giving one's whole life to, whatever the cost, it must be both certainly true and remarkably beneficial.

Many Christians in developed countries go about their days with no worries or fears of state-sanctioned persecution. But many Christians all over the world—both today and throughout history—have been faced with a decision: give up loyalty to Jesus or give up everything else. If Jesus were simply a good teacher or even a paramount moral example, the decision would be easy: give up loyalty to him and keep your life and all its blessings. If he were more than that, though—if he were God himself and the source of all of our future hope, then the decision would still be easy, and yet wholly different: give up your life now and receive from him untold blessings and joy for all eternity. And which decision you should make hinges on whether or not Jesus actually came back from the dead.

Conclusion

At the very least, I hope the importance of Jesus's resurrection has been made abundantly clear. Of course, proving that it actually happened is another thing entirely, and that's what the next section of this book aims to do. But if nothing else, my hope is that we can at least agree that if there is even the slightest chance that someone came back from the dead, we owe it to ourselves to be absolutely certain whether or not he actually did. Until we exhaust every source and every possibility, we shouldn't be satisfied.

The resurrection of Jesus is far too significant for us to remain in a place in which we think he *might* have risen from the dead. For if he did, then he deserves our attention, our trust, and our loyalty—truly our whole life. If he did not, then why bother worrying about him at all? That's the logic of the apostle Paul. "If in Christ we have hope in this life only, we are of all people most to be pitied."[5] In other words, if we're spending time worrying about Jesus and it only matters for our short time in this life, then we're wasting our time, and we should be pitied more than anyone. Following Jesus is either eternally rewarding or laughably futile, and which one depends on whether or not he did as he claimed he would do: resurrect. So we now begin our investigation into whether or not he did just that.

Chapter 3
Considering Atheism

We have to remember that what we observe is not nature herself, but nature exposed to our method of questioning.

—*Werner Heisenberg*

Now that we've argued for the importance of proving the significance of Jesus's resurrection as a historical event, let's move on to establish the philosophical possibility of such an event occurring. In particular, we need to agree on the possibility of a supernatural event occurring. For many, the consideration of the resurrection ends before it even begins, because there is no reason to consider the historical accuracy of an event that simply "cannot happen." Appealing to natural law, a skeptic may claim that it is foolish to even entertain the idea that a man came back from the dead.

There are, categorically speaking, two types of people who have trouble believing in a literal resurrection. The first type is the atheist. I use that term not pejoratively, but precisely. I mean simply what the word means: *a*, the Greek prefix for *not*, + *theos*, the Greek word for *god*, = *a-theos*, or *atheist*, meaning *no god*. Traditionally, someone who subscribes to an atheistic worldview claims to operate solely according to what scientific discovery has proved. They deny the possibility of any event that cannot be explained by natural law, and they argue that any spirituality or supernatural aspect to existence is merely fanciful. In fact, they deny (or at least should deny, if they are consistent with their worldview) any kind of spiritual dimension to the world—no souls, no fate, no higher power, no design, and no greater purpose. They believe the universe fell into being and has progressed randomly ever since. Richard Dawkins, ethologist and biologist, sums up the atheist's worldview like this: "In a universe of . . . blind physical forces and genetic replication, some people are going to get hurt, other people are going to get lucky, and you won't find any rhyme or reason in it, nor any justice. The universe we observe has precisely the properties we should expect if there is, at bottom, no design, no purpose, no evil, no good, nothing but pitiless indifference."[6]

The atheist's worldview suggests that everything has a strictly physical composition, made up of the same building blocks that were present at the initial explosion and expansion of the universe. This is the worldview we'll address in this chapter. Even if you do not hold to this belief, I believe this chapter will be beneficial nonetheless.

A False Dichotomy

First, we must address a common misconception. Faith and science often get pitted against each another as enemies. Many assume that having faith in God means you must reject scientific discoveries, or vice versa—that accepting the findings of the scientific community means you must reject any notion of the divine or supernatural. That is simply not the case. The belief in or acknowledgment of creative events or processes such as the Big Bang or evolution do not automatically presuppose an atheistic worldview. In fact, neither of those particular theories was initially posed as an alternative to intelligent design. Even today, they are widely purported as divine processes through which a design was implemented. Many Christians accept scientific findings of the modern era. They believe that the creator could have employed any number of creative methods that allowed for natural law to be the driving force behind what he created. So to say, for instance, "I don't believe in God because I believe the theory of evolution is true" is illogical. The two are not mutually exclusive.

To be fair, the origins of this fallacy are understandable. For much of human history, across all cultures, "the gods did it" was the sweeping answer for anything that was unexplainable. Divine intervention was the reason given for anything that escaped the level of understanding at the time. If a disease broke out, it was the will of the gods, who were obviously displeased. The stars in the sky were actually celestial beings waging war on one another. But all of this changed with the dawn of modern scientific discovery. Out of the Renaissance and, more concretely, the Enlightenment, the scientific method was born. People began to seek to understand why the world behaved the way it did. Things became measurable, mysteries were conquered, and human intellect flourished. The inevitable consequence of this wealth of scientific commitment and discovery was the growing sense that belief in God suggested ignorance or a lack of education. The pervading sentiment was that scientists figure things out, and people not smart enough to do so just believe God does it all. Thus, the ever-unfortunate false dichotomy between science and faith was born.

I say "unfortunate dichotomy" because, in reality, it's not a dichotomy at all, but rather a marriage. Let's consider the creation account of Genesis 1, for example—a commonly discussed matter in this conversation. The chapter is a beautifully poetic and artistic account illustrating how God set up this world to be orderly and "good." The logical progression of the days of creation (creating realms during the first three and filling those realms, respectively, in the next three) and the repetitive literary structure are the author's way of showing that this world was meant to be ruled by order, not disorder—by law, not chaos. So in fact, the picture it paints actually *supports* the scientific method. The only way something can be measurable is if it behaves the same way under the same circumstances every time it's observed. It must behave according to the laws to which it is subjected. If there was no natural law, something for which the Bible makes a case, there would be no way someone could ever truly measure or quantify anything.

Science is, by definition, "knowledge or a system of knowledge covering general truths or the operation of general laws especially as obtained and tested through scientific method."[7] How can you have a systematic endeavor without things operating according to a system? How can you test things unless you believe they will act the same way each time? How can you use samples to form conclusions unless you believe them to be accurately representative? The entire foundation of the scientific method is based on the presupposition that the universe operates according to, on some level, law and order. To say "when x happens, we can expect y" is an assumption that an event will occur in the same manner and according to the same properties as it did the last time. And so, rather than seeing an intelligent designer as an opposition to the reliability of scientific research, it is much more intellectually consistent to see one as a *reason* for it.

Science is contained to what it can measure. There is no reason why measuring and testing that which exists means it could not have been created. Science is not a force that accomplishes things on its own. It is the process of human beings performing tests and measurements on that which already exists. To say that the ability to test and measure the natural world rules out the possibility of it having a divine origin is, again, illogical.

Science as a Divine Gift

Taking the marriage of science and faith a step further, it's reasonable to argue that the ability we possess to make observations about the universe is actually proof of a higher purpose and design to the universe. In their book *The Privileged Planet*, analytic philosopher Jay W. Richards and astrobiologist Guillermo Gonzales argue that the same factors necessary for sustaining complex life are remarkably correlated to the factors necessary for scientific discovery. In other words, the same things that allow life to survive on Earth are the very things required to allow us, as observers on Earth, to make discoveries about our universe. The visible light spectrum, our location in the galaxy, our location in the solar system, the type of star we orbit, the composition of our atmosphere, the size of our planet, the size of our moon—all these things are among the factors necessary for intelligent life to survive on a planet. They also are required to allow for the observation and exploration of the universe *from* that planet. The statistical odds of such an overlap are staggeringly small, even when granting the enormity of our known universe. It's reasonable to assume, then, that one of the reasons we were given the opportunity to survive on what truly is a privileged planet is so we could have the opportunity to engage in scientific discovery. Understanding this correlation allows us to see that scientific discovery is not in opposition *to God* but is itself a gift given to us *by God*.

In fact, many of the fathers of modern science (e.g., Copernicus, Galileo, Isaac Newton, Charles Darwin, and others) viewed science in this way—as a gift given by their creator to discover truths about the world. They believed they were making discoveries and observations that explained the mind and methods of God—of an intelligent designer. Here's how Darwin put it in *On the Origin of Species*: "I should infer from analogy that probably all the organic beings which have ever lived on this earth have descended from some one primordial form, into which *life was first breathed by the Creator*" (emphasis added).[8]

Whether or not you agree with all of Darwin's conclusions, the fact remains that he didn't view his work as a way to supplant the genius of God, but rather as a way to support it. The same can be said for the other fathers of modern science mentioned above.

The opposition that such men faced from the institutional

structures of the church often gives the impression that they were set out to disprove the existence and necessity of God, when in fact they were actually seeking the ways in which God intended the universe and this world to function. It is a great irony, indeed, that scientific discovery, on the shoulders of such giants, is wrongfully categorized as a godless endeavor, when it was often the love of God and the desire to discover his methods that drove these individuals. In a very real sense, their work was their worship.

It is clear, however, that scientific inquiry is not always categorized as it once was. Both scientists and members of the general public often think of science as a means of explaining things for which a divine explanation is considered unsatisfactory and archaic. But when we get into the actual facts and figures regarding our origin and existence, we begin to see that the divine explanation isn't the one that's unsatisfactory.

A Finely Tuned Universe

Certain forces in our universe are known as physical constants or fundamental constants. These are forces that are not dependent on any other factor; they haven't developed over time. They simply are. And they always have been since the onset of the universe. Some of these include the following:

- gravitational force
- speed of light
- strong nuclear force
- weak nuclear force
- electromagnetic force
- mass of subatomic particles (e.g., protons)

- Planck's constant
- Boltzmann's constant [9]

Each of these constants (along with several others) is absolutely essential for the presence of life in a universe. What's more, many are essential for the presence of a physical universe. If even one of these values were tweaked ever so slightly, life as we know it could not exist. And yet every one of them is precisely what is needed in order for the universe to exist and accommodate life. This phenomenon is known as the finely tuned universe. That means that since all of the constants are perfect, they must have been tuned to their values. In other words, from a mathematical standpoint, it's as if someone dialed in all the correct values before the origin of the universe. Given the infinite number of possibilities for combinations and permutations of these constants, I (and many within the scientific community) would argue that the belief that our universe just happened to fall into place the way it did by chance is an untenable position. Even astronomers and physicists who deny the existence of God recognize this, and they admit there must be an alternative. Since many refuse to acknowledge the possibility of supernatural causation, three common responses to this quandary have emerged in popular science.

1. Multiverse theory

The multiverse theory suggests that our universe is not unique in its existence and that there is an infinite number of parallel universes in other dimensions. If an infinite number of universes exist, then at some point, the infinitely small probability of getting all the necessary components for continued existence could, perhaps, happen by chance. In other words, no probability is too small if you have unlimited chances to achieve it. So rather than the existence of one universe—our universe—an infinite number of universes exist in non-discoverable, unobservable dimensions, and it just so happens that our universe was the one roll of the dice that landed in such a way that complex life could be possible.

However, this theory fails to address two significant issues. First, it does not offer an explanation for the origin of all of these universes. Even if there were an infinite number of universes, from whence did they come? Remove a divine agent, and the origin of any number of universes, whether one or an infinite number of them, is still perplexing. Second, and more important, this theory is not scientific since it is not a testable hypothesis. By definition, if these parallel universes exist in other dimensions, there is no way we can ever confirm their existence. Proponents of this theory would say that the notion of a divine being is fanciful because it can't be observed or tested. It's clear then that this theory also falls short of their own standards.

2. Simulated reality

Recently, another theory regarding the origin of our universe has begun to garner support. More frequently, scientists are admitting that the possibility of randomly and accidentally achieving our universe's life-sustaining measurements is too small to consider, even if we are one chance among many others. What's more, there are many things in our universe that are too symmetrical, too complex, too precise—indeed, too perfect—to be formed accidentally, even with endless attempts. This has led many scientists to agree that the universe must have been, in fact, designed.

Physicists and astronomers, including popular astrophysicist Neil deGrasse Tyson and Tesla's CEO Elon Musk, have begun to support the possibility that our universe is nothing more than the product of a simulation run by a species far more advanced than ours. Of course, that would easily account for the finely tuned requirements for sustaining life that exist in our cosmos.

One glaringly obvious problem with this hypothesis is that those who propose it are still left with a problem of origin. In logic, this is known as an infinite regress. The proposition is true only if we assume that a prior condition—a previous proposition—is true, but we can never arrive at the original source. The only way we can assume our universe is simulated is if a previous universe, which was simulated perfectly enough to sustain complex life, eventually developed the technology to simulate our universe. Who, then, simulated the universe prior to that one? Hopefully, the fallacy is clear. Eventually, we must reach a life form in a universe that is not simulated. There must be an original, but from whence did it come? How did it form perfectly to sustain life? The simple question "What came before _____?" makes the simulation theory's problems apparent.

The second problem with this theory is not theoretical but logical. If we are in a simulated reality, there would be no way to ever know. It's purely conjecture, and it could never be anything more. Every notion that we have of sentience would be fake. We would only ever know what our simulators want us to know. And so, like the multiverse theory, this is hardly a scientific proposition. It's not a hypothesis. It's not testable or observable, and it never could be.

3. Top-down cosmology

Top-down cosmology is perhaps the most complex of the explanations for our finely tuned universe. Originally suggested by Stephen Hawking and his colleague Thomas Hertog, this view suggests that the universe does not have just one history but rather many different histories under many different sets of restraints, and that only one option, that is, our current one, survived. Another way to think of it is similar to the multiverse theory, in that many different universes existed at the time of the Big Bang and that only one survived because it happened to have the proper constants necessary to sustain time and space.

Obviously, Hawking is a brilliant man, and his cosmological work is renowned, but with his theory, we run into the very same gap in logic as we did with the multiverse theory and the notion of a simulated reality. This isn't technically scientific hypothesis; it's conjecture aimed at removing the need for a divine agent for creation. It leaves us in the same place as the previous two theories: it provides no tangible evidence or even a means of seeking evidence. There are no data to support it, and there never can be. If other universes existed in various dimensions at some point in the past and no longer do today, there is no way we will ever know. Yet again, for some reason, this theory is viewed as more scientific and modern than the concept of God as a creator.

It is worth noting, however, that Hawking admits elsewhere that the universe as we know it, originating solely from the Big Bang (that is, without any divine design and guidance), is a difficult position to hold. He stated, "The odds against a universe like ours coming out of something like the Big Bang are enormous. I think there are clearly religious implications."[10] To then say that an event such as the Big Bang was able to produce multiple universes (of which only ours survived), each with its own unique physical constraints, doesn't remove the "religious implications" in the slightest.

Faith of a Different Kind

Let's set aside for a moment the scientific problems with all these theories and make a sweeping point regarding their shared logical fallacy. These theories (and those similar to them) are beyond physical observation. They are, instead, metaphysical (transcending physical matter or the laws of nature) in their essence. That means that attempts to explain the universe's existence and ability to sustain life apart from one metaphysical explanation (intelligent design) have led to explanations that rely on metaphysical explanations.

At some level, whether by some form of parallel universes or the simulation of this universe, we must put our faith in that which is unseen. The question, then, becomes this: Why is one metaphysical option more scientific than the other? If science is the observation of what exists, then the proposition of infinite parallel universes in other dimensions—dimensions that can never be observed—is hardly scientific. The same can be said for the proposition that we are simply part of a highly advanced gaming simulation of another species. They are all, at their core, matters of faith.

We must ask ourselves, then, if the origin and structure of the universe can only be explained by unobservable, untestable means, and what makes one suggestion more tenable than the other. What makes the multiverse theory more valid or more scientific than the belief in a supernatural creator? Is it easier to accept that we are nothing more than the virtual product of a higher species' hard drive? If so, why? Why are many so quick to dismiss the notion of God because there's no proof but will jump at the opportunity to believe other theories that are absent any proof or even the possibility of acquiring proof in the future? Indeed, they have laid aside the scientific method for a faith-based conclusion. The irony is heightened by the fact that the more the evidence is thoroughly considered, the more likely a supernatural, omnipotent creator—God—becomes.

Complex Life

The origin of life

Let's move on now from the origin of the universe to the origin of its crown jewel—complex life. No question has puzzled modern scientists more than this: From whence did life come? How can the inanimate progress into the sentient? Several theories have been put forth in an attempt to answer that question.

One common theory is that life must have been seeded here by an extraterrestrial form of intelligent life. Many deniers of theistic intelligent design concede this alternative.

They concede that the necessary building blocks for life are too complex to have sprung up spontaneously from inanimate materials and thus suggest that the necessary components for complex life to evolve must have been seeded here at some point in our planet's past. We don't need to stretch our minds to spot the logical inconsistency here. We run into the same problem as the simulated universe hypothesis. If the building blocks of life are too complex to spontaneously form complex organisms, then they could not have done so elsewhere in the universe any more easily than they could have on Earth. If life *was* put here, *who* put it here? Presumably, another form of complex life. Then who put that form of complex life on its planet of origin? Who seeded the complex life that seeded the complex life on Earth? We have another infinite regress fallacy. At some point, we must concede that a being of not only higher intelligence but higher—even supernatural—power created the necessary components for complex life. If life was put here or put anywhere else in the universe, it must have, at some point, been put here or there by a being capable of designing and creating from nothing—creating *ex nihilo*, or "out of nothing."

The only other possibility that life was seeded on Earth from an external source is that life spontaneously originated here on Earth, with only the materials present on Earth. Within this broader theory, several subtheories exist, and most have one thing in common: amino acids—the building blocks of life. According to these theories, somehow, whether by electric spark or within a primordial soup, naturally forming amino acids combined in such a way to produce the first self-replicating cell, leading to ribonucleic acid (RNA). In what is often referred to as an RNA world, RNA began to perform all of the basic functions necessary for molecules to reproduce and eventually evolve and combine to form cells with membranes. If this were to happen, then theoretically, multi-cell simple organisms could form and subsequently evolve, beginning a process that could lead to complex life. The only problem (and a rather prominent problem) with this theory is that no one knows how this could have happened. No scientist has been able to show (or even suggest) exactly how RNA could have begun to exist. The late Robert Shapiro, a former chemist at New York University, stated, "The appearance of such a molecule, given the way chemistry functions, is incredibly improbable. It would be a once-in-a-universe long shot. To adopt this [view], you have to believe we were incredibly lucky." [11]

Once more, we have faith being put in an unobservable and extremely unlikely process. Scientists who deny intelligent design have no idea how a molecule simple enough to come from inanimate materials yet complex enough to self-replicate and evolve could have begun to exist. "It simply happened," is as much as anyone can say. Again, we have to wonder if a scientific worldview is opposed to a theistic worldview based on the claim that a scientific worldview is centered on evidence and facts. Why should we accept a theory as scientific if it has no evidence or factual support? If intelligent design is indefensible because it cannot be proved or because it ventures outside of observable reality, then any existing alternative explanation of the origin of life on Earth should be deemed equally difficult to defend.

The sustaining of life

Although we've already looked at some of the factors necessary to sustain complex life on a planet, a more extensive list is worth examining. Assuming the origin of life hurdle has somehow been cleared, there still remains the fact that even in our expansive universe, the probability of a planet being able to sustain complex life (by accident) is miniscule. Many of us have probably heard of the Goldilocks zone, the area in a solar system where a planet is not too close or too far but just the right distance from its sun. While this orbital "sweet spot" is rare indeed, there are many other factors necessary to sustain complex life, including the following:

- correct location in the galaxy
- planetary system with giant planets (such as Jupiter and Saturn) to shield inner planets
- orbiting the right kind of star (not too cool or too hot)
- correct sized moon to stabilize a habitable axis
- correct type of planet (terrestrial)
- perfect thickness of the planet's crust to maintain plate tectonic activity
- circulating a liquid iron core to generate a magnetic field
- oxygen-rich atmosphere
- enough liquid water
- correct ratio of water to land (and correct separation of that land into continents) [12]

This list isn't comprehensive, but it does give us an idea of how detailed the factors are. Even if we assign a very

Considering Atheism

generous probability to each of these factors, the chance of all of these occurring at the same time—on the same planet—is staggeringly small.

Multiplied probabilities

Here is the bottom line. To believe that complex life arose on Earth through purely material circumstances is to believe in the most astronomical of improbabilities. Let's consider each step in the sequence:

- The finely tuned forces necessary to sustain the existence of the universe are so unlikely to have occurred that without acknowledging the supernatural, one must accept a nearly infinitely small statistical probability.
- The statistical probability of the circumstances necessary for a self-replicating, evolving molecule to form into a cell from purely inanimate materials is, as well, nearly infinitely small.
- The factors necessary to sustain complex life on Earth are so numerous that to believe all fell into place is, again, to accept an almost infinitely small statistical probability.

To get the probability of two events occurring simultaneously, you multiply their individual probabilities. For instance, if one event has a 50% chance of occurring and another event has the same probability, the likelihood that both will happen is 25% (0.5 x 0.5 = 0.25, or 5/10 x 5/10 = 25/100 = 25%). That means the likelihood of very improbable events occurring together shrinks exponentially.

Consider three events that have a 1% chance each:

$$1/100 \times 1/100 \times 1/100 = 1/1,000,000$$

Three events at just 1% each have a one in a million chance of occurring all together. Imagine how small the chances are for three events to occur that each one has a one in a million chance of happening, then. Or, don't imagine. It's 1/1,000,000,000,000,000,000—that's one in a quintillion. And what if each event had a one in quintillion chance, or if each had a nearly infinitely small probability? What if you multiplied three probabilities together, each with a seemingly endless string of zeros on the bottom? Functionally, you approach zero. That is what it looks like to suggest that all of the factors in the universe and on our planet not only allowed for but somehow accidentally created complex organisms. The probability is virtually nonexistent. There is no number that you and I can fathom to put on the bottom of that fraction that could communicate the unlikelihood of the above events happening without a supernatural explanation. In comparison, the chances of not winning every lottery every year for the rest of your life is an absolute assurance. But I wonder how many people who discourage others from spending their life's savings on lottery tickets also advocate for staking their eternity on probabilities remarkably smaller than even the most unlikely lottery win.

The Appearance of Design

Setting aside the mathematical improbability of our universe and the life therein originating by happenstance, we must also consider the remarkable intricacy and complexity of life as it exists in its current form. Specifically, we need to consider what many scientists and philosophers, even ones that subscribe to an atheistic worldview, call, in some way or another, the appearance of design. The idea is that even a cursory survey of the life forms on this planet, both as individuals and as parts in a working whole, leads to the conclusion that this world is (or at least appears to be) purposefully designed. Below are a few relevant quotes from notable atheists:

> If anything is true about nature, it is that plants and animals seem intricately and almost *perfectly designed* for living their lives.... Nature resembles a well-oiled machine, with every species an intricate cog or gear. ... The more one learns about plants and animals, the more one marvels at how well their *designs* fit their ways of life (emphasis added). –Jerry Coyne [13]

> The design inference comes naturally. The reason people think that a Designer created the world is because it *looks* designed (emphasis in original). –Michael Shermer [14]

> Yet the living results of natural selection overwhelmingly impress us with the *appearance of design* as if by a master watchmaker, impress us with the *illusion of design and planning* (emphasis added). –Richard Dawkins [15]

> A common sense interpretation of the facts suggests that a *superintellect* has monkeyed with the physics,

as well as with chemistry and biology. . . . The numbers one calculates from the facts seem to me so overwhelming as to put this conclusion almost beyond question (emphasis added). –Fred Hoyle[16]

A quick Internet search will turn up many other quotes and similar ideas. It is clear that whether someone suggests the universe is actually designed or not, admitting that it gives the appearance of being designed is unavoidable.

All of our quoted atheists would most likely agree with the statement that the aim of scientific discovery is to draw conclusions based on what is seen, observed, and measured. They all have also admitted that when one sees, observes, and measures the world, the data and evidence point to it being *designed*—to a *designer*. Thus to deny the existence of an intelligent designer is to draw conclusions in direct opposition to what one sees, observes, and measures—the very fallacy of which atheists often accuse theists. I hope it is becoming clear that it is not the theists who deny the evidence.

Why Atheism?

I once had the privilege of speaking at my alma mater's baccalaureate ceremony. After tossing aside what seemed like scores of ideas for a topic, I landed on a simple concept—a single request to the graduating students. I implored them, "Before you make a decision, especially an important one, always articulate your reasons for making it." Surveying our motivations behind a particular decision often reveals much about the decision itself. So at this point, if the impossibility of the supernatural—the spiritual—

is still something you're absolutely certain of, I would ask that you pause and ask yourself this question: Why? Is the supernatural impossible because a purely physical explanation to the existence of the universe and the complex life therein makes the most sense? Given what we know from scientific discovery, that would be a difficult case to make. Or is there another reason? Perhaps it's worth asking whether the data are shaping your beliefs or whether your beliefs are shaping the data. Richard Lewontin, an atheist, admits that he and many of his colleagues accept certain scientific conclusions, not because the conclusion itself is tenable but because the worldview to which they have committed themselves compels them to do so. Lewontin wrote in his "Billions and Billions of Demons," a review of Carl Sagan's book *The Demon-Haunted World: Science as a Candle in the Dark*:

> We . . . take the side of science *in spite* of the patent absurdity of some of its constructs, *in spite* of its failure to fulfill many of its extravagant promises of health and life, *in spite* of the tolerance of the scientific community for unsubstantiated just-so stories, because we have a prior commitment, a commitment to materialism. It is not that the methods and institutions of science somehow compel us to accept a material explanation of the phenomenal world, but, on the contrary, that we are forced by our *a priori* adherence to material causes to create an apparatus of investigation and a set of concepts that produce material explanations, no matter how counter-intuitive, no matter how mystifying to the uninitiated. Moreover, that materialism is an

absolute, for we cannot allow a Divine Foot in the door" (emphases in original).[17]

I greatly appreciate his candor. He says "we are forced by our *a priori* adherence to material causes" to argue for particular theories. An *a priori* adherence is just as it sounds, a prior adherence—a prior commitment. The decision that the universe and life therein must have strictly material causes comes first, and then the data are interpreted and theories are suggested in such a way that supports the prior decision. This way of approaching an issue stands in direct opposition to the basic framework of the scientific method. Nevertheless, it pervades the scientific community so deeply that it is difficult to imagine how the cycle could ever be broken.

It's worth noting once again that this is the very type of reasoning of which theists are often accused. Most people, if asked, would say that it is religious people who try to make the evidence fit their pre-existing beliefs. When the evidence is considered objectively, though, we find that the opposite is often true. The evidence points directly to a supernatural intelligent designer, and it is those who deny the existence of such that do all they can to make the evidence appear to support their positions.

That is why the question "Why?" is so crucial. The denial of a divine creator is usually less a matter of logical deduction and more a matter of false assumptions. People often assume that a theistic worldview and modern scientific discoveries are incompatible; but they are not. People often assume that there are logically sound answers to the existence of the universe and complex life that do not include the need for an intelligent designer; but there are not. People often assume that belief in an intelligent designer precludes a commitment to reason; but it does not. All in all, we must admit that a sound case can be made that modern scientific discovery and reason together point to a theistic worldview.

I hardly expect the content in this chapter to be sufficient to convince everyone who denies the existence of God to immediately believe otherwise. I am hopeful, however, that it has sufficiently raised enough questions to lead you, at the very least, to reconsider your absolute certainty that there is no divine or spiritual presence in the universe, if that is a position you currently hold. Because if it is at all possible that a merely physical explanation is inadequate, then we owe it to ourselves to commit every ounce of intellectual capacity to answer this question: "What is the alternative?" For what could be more worth our time than the consideration that God exists and that we thus have a higher purpose? If there is a creator, then as his creation, we owe it to ourselves to exhaust every possibility when it comes to our relationship with him.

> *If there is a creator, then as his creation, we owe it to ourselves to exhaust every possibility when it comes to our relationship with him.*

Chapter 4
Considering Agnosticism

Christianity . . . is either the most devastating disclosure of the deepest reality in the world, or it's a sham, a nonsense. . . . Most of us, unable to cope with saying either of those things, condemn ourselves to live in the shallow world in between.
—N. T. Wright

If you use terms such as *faith*, *spirit*, or *soul*, if you have made some mention of a higher being or higher power, whether a personified universe or fate or a divine presence of some sort, then this is the chapter is for you. You most likely believe that people have, to some extent, a spiritual nature or soul but might not be quite sure what that looks like or what the implications are. You most likely acknowledge some aspect of existence—namely, human existence—that is not strictly material. If you relate to any of these descriptions, you likely identify as an agnostic. Unlike atheists, agnostics admit there is some form of supernatural presence in the universe but add a caveat to that admission with the fact that it is unknown and unknowable. I believe, though, that if an agnostic person remains consistent with his or her worldview, he or she will acknowledge the legitimate possibility of Jesus actually rising from the dead.

Admittedly, the task before me in this chapter is much easier than the task in the previous chapter, which required research into several fields of study. Now, the arguments are strictly logical. What follows is a very simple case of "if *A*, then *B*; if *B*, then *C*." Our starting point is the acknowledgment of some sort of spiritual presence or higher purpose in the universe, even if the details of that recognition are vague. Our end point, as I hope to show, is the recognition that a supernatural event—namely, a physical resurrection—lies very much within the confines of reason: if one, then the other. And here's why.

A Design Means a Designer

First, we must consider the matter of design. There are ultimately two possibilities about the world we live in. Either there is some element of design and purpose or everything is pure happenstance. Either there is a reason for the way things are or there is no reason at all except "that's simply the way it happened." Usually, spiritual people prefer the former option over the latter. A sense of higher purpose gives hope; it means we are not merely a highly unlikely combination of raw materials living inconsequential lives that are nothing more than chains of chemical reactions. The implication is obvious, though. If we are not merely accidental—if there is something to our existence other than random chance—then there *is* a purpose. There is, indeed, a design.

If there is a design, then the conclusion that follows is that there is a designer. We cannot have something intentionally formed without it being formed by someone who can exercise intentionality. If the universe is subject to a higher purpose, then there must be a being who was able to implement that purpose. Thus, choosing to believe in some aspect of spirituality is consequential to believing in a divine, supernatural being—God.

If there is, in fact, a divine designer, then answering the following questions is quite simple: "Who is the designer? What kind of being is capable of catalyzing the design and creation of the universe? What kind of higher power can design and implement physical and natural laws? Who can fine-tune the universe to the exact specifications necessary to sustain complex organisms? Who can make something out of nothing and lead that something to produce sentient life? Surely, this being would have to be powerful—even all-powerful. What limitations of power can we impose on a being who can create from nothing? With the presence of a design or higher purpose inevitably comes the presence of a designer—a divine, all-powerful being. If one, then the other. In other words, the belief in any kind of design or purpose in this life is synonymous with the belief in an omnipotent creator.

The Source of the Metaphysical

Similar to the matter of design and purpose is the issue of spirituality itself. As already mentioned, spiritual people believe there is some aspect of human existence that is not merely physical, whether it's a belief in the human soul, the human spirit, moral laws, the greater good, and so on. All those terms imply that there is something that is intertwined with our existence that could not have simply appeared through strictly material means. In other words, the spiritual aspect of our existence could not have begun at some later point *after* the creation of the universe.

Then from whence did spirituality come? Clearly, we can say that humans did not evolve into having a soul. At no point could there have been a particular chemical reaction or atomic combination that resulted in something metaphysical. One cannot create that which is non-physical from that which is purely physical. If there is *any* spiritual aspect—soul, objective morality, and so forth—it had to be there from the beginning. Atoms don't make a soul. A true sense of morality cannot be created in a lab with raw materials. The only answer is that someone put those spiritual aspects in place, implanting them into our existence from the onset. To acknowledge the existence of a soul, a spirit, or anything else that does not have an atomic structure is to acknowledge the existence of a designer—a cosmic author—who created them as part of our nature.

> One cannot create that which is non-physical from that which is purely physical.

Not only must we acknowledge the presence of a divine being, but we must also grant that this being's power is beyond our comprehension and ability to measure. We cannot reasonably put limitations on the power of a being capable of creating both spiritual and physical dimensions. And if we say that there is such a being—God—capable of not only creating us but also ingraining into us a spiritual aspect and dimension, then we are admitting that he is powerful enough and capable enough to do anything that escapes our sense of logic and rationale. If this God exists, then his ability to cause a supernatural event (e.g., a resurrection) is hardly unreasonable. In fact, it's an absolute certainty.

Objective Morality

I argued above that a sense of morality is intertwined with the spiritual aspect of human existence. Some might give pause to this claim, asserting that humanity does not need a spiritual dimension to know right from wrong or good from evil, which is an assertion worth briefly addressing.

If a sense of good or right does not come from a creator's design and is not based on his moral will, then where could it come from? What can serve as a "true north" for morality if not something external from and transcendent over us? Several options have been entertained throughout the history of moral philosophy.

Some would say that what is good is whatever maximizes health and happiness for the largest number of people—or to phrase it in the negative, whatever minimizes suffering and sadness for the largest number of people. But we might ask whose definition of *happiness* we are using, or whose definition of *suffering*? Certainly, no one would say that everyone can be protected from harm, so how do we decide who gets protected and who is helped? Whose health and happiness should come at the expense of others?

"Well," one might argue, "we figure that out collectively. Whatever definition of 'good' and 'bad' that most people agree on is the working definition." But then, who are "most people"? The "most people" from everyone who has ever lived? The "most people" alive today? The "most people" alive today in our own immediate context and culture? Is it subjectively based on culture and context? Does our modern Western view of morality apply to all peoples and all cultures for all time? And what if the majority holds a view with which someone strongly disagrees? What grounds does that person have to disagree? If the majority rules, so to speak, then to disagree with the majority is to be "wrong."

What right, then, would someone have to visit a culture and speak against its accepted practices? Could we visit a people group that openly practices infanticide and condemn their actions? As a culture, they have decided what is morally acceptable, have they not? "But, it's just wrong!" many would say. Indeed, it is. But on what grounds do we make that claim? "We just know it is, instinctively." Again, I agree. We do. But how? What is it that gives human beings a unique ability to sense right from wrong? When did the human conscience deviate from all other instincts in the animal kingdom? What drives us to defend and help the poor, the sick, and the marginalized? Certainly, we cannot point to anything physical or natural. Apart from humans, the whole natural order is predicated on taking advantage of the weak and defenseless. And most of us would say that's wrong. But why? In order for there to be any sense of morality that stands apart from the rest of the animal kingdom, it must be sourced from something other than natural causes. It must be non-natural. It must be *super*natural. And that means it must come from a supernatural presence—from God.

Some Supernatural?

The conclusion is clear: if we are to say that there is *any* higher purpose, *any* design, or *any* spirituality in the universe—

if we have souls, if we are capable of true love, if beauty is not merely an objective combinations of ratios, if we can truly know right from wrong—then there must be an intelligent designer. God must exist. Discerning his nature, his character, and his will for the world is another matter that we'll address later. But what we should agree on is that the presence of any of these things means the existence of an all-powerful creator.

For now, though, let's ask ourselves this: If there *is* an all-powerful creator, how can we deny the possibility of a supernatural occurrence? Or to put it another way, if we acknowledge a creator's ability to design and create an entire universe, why would we doubt his ability to intervene in the events of that universe? We cannot reasonably concede that there is a being who can create from nothing and simultaneously deny that he does not exercise authority and control over that which he created. We cannot pick and choose which kinds and categories of supernatural we are comfortable with. If we acknowledge that there is a God who can design and create a universe, it makes little sense to say that we understand precisely in which ways he is free to exercise his power. To say that the act of creating something from nothing is believable but the act of raising someone from the dead isn't is contradictory. The acknowledgement of an all-powerful creator is explicitly the acknowledgment of the possibility of a supernatural occurrence in our world. And the acknowledgment of the possibility of the supernatural is a clear concession that a literal resurrection could have occurred on Earth.

The spiritual, agnostic person is left, then, with two options. First, that person can decide to deny the possibility of a resurrection, and in so doing, abandon all language of souls and spirits, refuse any mention of an objective morality, and give up the right to believe in any higher purpose, fate, or the like. In other words, that person must become utterly atheistic, claiming that everything that has ever occurred is the remarkably unlikely, accidental result of a random and exceedingly lucky collocation of molecules. It is my hope that after reading the previous chapter, this option seems less favorable, even untenable. Second, that person can, along with a belief in a human soul and a higher purpose, acknowledge that a bodily resurrection is possible. There is no logical middle ground between those two options. If there is no supernatural dimension to our existence, then of course we ought to deny even the possibility of a supernatural event. But we must also deny any other mentions of the supernatural and its implications. If there *is* a supernatural aspect to our existence, then the door swings wide open for the possibility of occurrences that are outside what we have come to know as the natural order—such as a resurrection.

Conclusion

As I stated before, I do not believe one chapter of one book will sufficiently *cause* a change of worldview for every reader. What I hope it can do, however, is catalyze one. Most people do not spend time considering the logical implications of their worldviews, but I believe it is of the utmost importance that we do so. What could be more important than finding out the truth about our existence? It takes either an overconfident or extremely indifferent person (perhaps both) to never worry about matters of higher purpose and eternity. Discovering the truth about our existence, though, requires thinking. We must think about how we answer questions regarding the origin of time and space. We must think about whether we accept or deny the presence of a spiritual dimension to our existence. If we accept it, we must ponder from whence it came. We must consider what we believe about our lives as human beings. Are we merely the consequence of a most fortuitous combination of atoms? Or are we something more?

I am convinced that if we do think carefully about these matters, we're left to conclude that a literal resurrection is entirely within the realm of possibility—that belief in a resurrection does not require the abandonment of critical thought, but is rather the product of it. However, if you are still not convinced that a resurrection could have occurred, I invite you to continue reading. Sometimes, different evidences speak differently to different people. Perhaps where philosophical and scientific arguments fall short, historical arguments will not. And that is where we return to now—to the historical evidence for the resurrection of Jesus.

PART II
THE EVIDENCE

Chapter 5
The Historical Documents

There's an old saying about those who forget history.
I don't remember it, but it's good.

—*Stephen Colbert*

How do we know that an event occurred in history? It was recorded. Today, that recording is likely by video cameras and cell phones, but for most of human history, that meant someone wrote it down. In fact, any event we don't witness can only be known by trusting the testimony of people who did witness it. Unless we say that reliable historical fact is confined only to what we see for ourselves, then at some point we will have to trust other people to reveal to us what truly happened at any given point in history. Of course, we can't trust all reports; we have to scrutinize their validity. We must hold the claims of others to a standard of proof rigorous enough for us to trust. Someone may easily write down that Abraham Lincoln was four feet tall. That person could even get that information published in a book. Does that make it true? Of course not! In order to be accepted as true, any piece of information must be corroborated by a sufficient number of independent witnesses who are deemed trustworthy. It must be recorded, and then it must be confirmed.

Since it is at least reasonable to accept the possibility of a supernatural event (e.g., a resurrection), we must keep that in mind as we turn to the historical data. If we say the documents are unreliable because they document supernatural events, we have committed a logical fallacy. Given the philosophical possibility of a supernatural event, we must allow the documents to speak for themselves. Their accuracy and reliability must fall under the same criteria that we use to scrutinize any historical document. If they record an event that someone refuses to believe, then the burden of proof is on the skeptic to prove that event definitively could not have happened. To say it could not have happened because it is supernatural is circular, insufficient reasoning. So as we approach the examination of the legitimacy of the documents in question and the information therein, we must remember not to place unsubstantiated presuppositions (e.g., the impossibility of the supernatural) on them.

The Gospel Accounts

The first documents worthy of consideration are the Gospel accounts written by the Four Evangelists: Matthew, Mark, Luke, and John. These four documents begin the New Testament, and they each explicitly record the resurrection of Jesus as a historical event. The question is, of course, are they trustworthy? While there are many considerations to make when examining the reliability of these accounts (or any historical document, for that matter), three are of primary importance:

1. genre of the material
2. time frame in which they were written
3. number of manuscripts reproduced

The reason the genre is important is quite simple. If something is not written as historical reportage, then any claims of a historical nature can be dismissed. If the Gospel accounts were written as fanciful myth or poetic legend and were never meant to be taken as historical information, then obviously they are not worthy of consideration. The time frame of their writing is also important. The more time that passes between the time of the actual events and the time they are written down, the higher the chance for perversion of the facts. The fewer degrees of separation between those who witnessed the events and those who wrote them down, the more reliable the documents are. Finally, the number of manuscripts is worthy of consideration because people only take the time to diligently reproduce documents if they are worth reproducing. Since anyone can write anything once, we must consider how many other sources corroborated the events and made copies.

Genre: History or myth?

What were the Gospel writers actually trying to accomplish? What were they trying to convey in their writings? Often, the Gospel accounts are placed in the same genre as the tales of Achilles or King Arthur—stories that may have been loosely tied to historical events but became so shrouded in legend that it is difficult to read their tales and know what is true and what is elaborated or even fabricated. But do they belong in that category? Should we approach the written accounts of Jesus the same way we approach the stories of Beowulf or Odysseus? Should we read the Gospels with a grain of salt, assuming that there is an intentional, entertaining mixture of truth and legend?

To help answer these questions, we'll turn again to one of the past century's foremost experts on ancient and medieval literature. Before he was a theologian, before he was even a Christian, C. S. Lewis was one of the world's leading literary scholars. He taught medieval literature at Oxford University and eventually became the chair of the Medieval and Renaissance Literature Department at Magdalen College at Cambridge University. Long before his conversion, he had an affinity for and masterful grasp of the history and form of literary genres. If there was ever an authority on categorizing ancient pieces of literature, it was Lewis. In his paper "Modern Theology and Biblical Criticism," Lewis shared his encounters with the Gospel accounts:

> I have been reading poems, romances, vision-literature, legends, myths all my life. I know what they are like. I know that not one of them is like this. Of this text there are only two possible views. Either this is reportage. . . . Or else, some unknown writer . . . without known predecessors, or successors, suddenly anticipated the whole technique of modern, novelistic, realistic narrative. If it [the Gospels] is untrue, it must be narrative of that kind. The reader who doesn't see this has simply not learned to read.[18]

Here's what Lewis is saying. To read the Gospels and assume they are not historical reportage is to not understand how to read ancient literature. To classify them as legend or myth is to misunderstand both the author's intent and the work itself because, as he argues, the manner in which they are written is not consistent with any other piece of literature that fits into ancient folklore or legend. For instance, we are told in John's Gospel that Peter caught 153 fish. Mark, in his Gospel account, not only reports that Jesus was asleep on a boat, but which part of the boat he was asleep on (the stern) and what he was sleeping on (a cushion). That type of detail is found nowhere in ancient legendary literature. It is only found in eyewitness reports of historical events. It is clear that an honest evaluation of the genre of the Gospels leads to a single conclusion: they were written and meant to be read as historical reortage.

We can even find internal evidence of this authorial intent within the Gospels themselves. For instance, Luke begins his Gospel this way:

> *Inasmuch as many have undertaken to compile a narrative of the things that have been accomplished among us, just as those who from the beginning were eyewitnesses and ministers of the word have delivered them to us, it seemed good to me also, having followed all things closely for some time past, to write an orderly account for you, most excellent Theophilus, that you may have certainty concerning the things you have been taught.*[19]

What does Luke tell us?

1. Other people have begun to compile narratives of what happened.
2. There were eyewitnesses to the events who passed on information to some of those who are writing these accounts.
3. This is going to be an "orderly account" because he has "followed all things closely."
4. The Gospel's goal is to give the reader certainty about the matters at hand.

This means that when Luke decided to write his Gospel, he didn't sit down at a desk and simply write a story that sounded cohesive or favorable. He did research. He asked people who were present at the events. He spoke with those closest to Jesus. Although Luke's style is more rigid and detail-oriented than the other Gospels, this is the manner in which all the Gospels were written.

Aside from the stylistic markers and internal evidence, we know that the Gospel accounts share in the traits that marked ancient Greco-Roman biographies. These biographies intended to recount the real accomplishments of real people, and were often between 10,000 and 20,000 words in length, written in continuous narrative prose.[20] What's more, they often don't follow a strict chronological structure, tending to primarily cover only a portion of the subject's life, putting even greater emphasis on the last week or so of the subject's life.[21] The Gospel accounts—the biographies of Jesus—follow this same pattern. It's clear that anyone reading these documents would have known they were meant to be read as historical, biographical reportage.

To be fair, confirming that the Gospel accounts were intended to be read as historical reportage is one thing; showing that they can actually be trusted as such is altogether another endeavor. "Okay," a skeptic could rebut, "I'll grant that the authors were writing historical reports, not legend, but how can we know what they wrote down is accurate? Surely, people have attempted to report history and failed, producing inaccurate accounts of events. Couldn't the Gospel authors simply have messed up and thought they were recording fact when, in actuality, they were recording fabricated information?" This is, indeed, a fair argument and one to which we'll now turn our attention.

Time frame: How soon after the events?

One of the primary criteria for determining the accuracy of historical documents is the length of time that passed between when the events occurred and when they were recorded. The more time that passes, the greater the chance of the accounts having inaccuracies and elaborations. The fewer degrees of separation between those who witnessed the events and those who wrote it down make the account more reliable. So the question at hand is how soon after the events of Jesus's life were the Gospels written?

Mark wrote the earliest Gospel account. The majority of modern textual scholarship puts the dating of Mark's account somewhere in the AD 60s. Even the latest datings of Mark's account reach only slightly into the early AD 70s, but the references to the not-yet-destroyed temple in Jerusalem (destroyed in AD 70 by the emperor Titus) makes a dating in the AD mid-60s favorable. Matthew and Luke wrote their accounts next, but only shortly after Mark wrote his. We know this because some of the material in Matthew and Luke is adopted from Mark's account, and internal evidence within the text also makes it most likely that it was written in the late AD 60s. However, even allowing for the latest possible date, one could not make a strong case for anything later than the AD 70s. Mark, Matthew, and Luke are known as the Synoptic Gospels, since their form, structure, and content are similar. All of these Gospel accounts were written within 30 to 40 years after the events they describe—during the lifetime of those who lived during the events and witnessed them.

John's Gospel account is, admittedly, quite different from the Synoptics. However, despite structural and stylistic differences, it carries ample credibility with regard to the time frame in which it was written. It has proved difficult for scholars to pinpoint a narrow range in which to place the date of composition. That said, however, based on internal evidence, the writing of John's Gospel could have been written as early as AD 50. Some scholars believe that John's Gospel makes it clear that he was working with the texts of Mark, Matthew, and Luke, and that a dating after AD 70 is more likely. Since it is likely the latest of the four Gospels, scholars have cautiously concluded that it could have been composed toward the end of the first century. All the external, extrabiblical evidence from that time period tells us that it was a universal consensus that John the apostle wrote the account himself, and therefore regardless of how late one dates the work, it must fall within his lifetime.

Given that there is sufficient evidence to date all of the

Gospel accounts within the lifetime of the eyewitnesses of the events and the apostles themselves, we can conclude with a high degree of certainty that the events recorded in the accounts are recorded accurately. The common claim that the stories of the Gospels developed into legends in the centuries following the actual life of Jesus is simply incompatible with the time frame in which we can place the composition of the accounts. They were simply written too early to have developed and evolved over the early life stages of the church.

Credibility: How many manuscripts?

At face value, the number of manuscripts doesn't necessarily seem like an important metric. "Couldn't the wrong information just be written down numerous times?" someone might ask. However, when we consider how information was passed from person to person and place to place in the ancient world, the number of copies created is an important point to consider.

In the ancient world, the number of manuscripts reproduced was directly correlated to the importance of the documents. Without any other way to transmit written material than writing it by hand, the copying of manuscripts was not an endeavor that was undertaken lightly. The sheer time that it took to painstakingly copy written material served as a gatekeeper of sorts against non-credible material. No one was going to waste time copying manuscripts of a work if that work was not considered worthy of being copied. Hence, the more manuscripts, the more likely it is that the material is important and factual.

There are more than 5,600 manuscripts of New Testament works in the original language. Compared to other works of classical literature, that number is staggeringly high. The next most copied piece of literature from antiquity is Homer's *Iliad* with 643 manuscripts, and even that number is large when compared to the 43 manuscripts of Plato's tetralogies and the seven manuscripts of any one work attributed to Aristotle. Do historians and scholars doubt the authorship and authenticity of the aforementioned works of Homer, Plato, and Aristotle? No. Yet, there are more than nine times the number of New Testament manuscripts compared to the next most prolifically copied work. That's not to say all the aforementioned works belong in the same genre (we've already discussed the differences between the Gospels and, say, Homer's *Iliad*), but it does go to show the importance of the Gospels compared to other ancient works.

Again, the number of copies alone does not provide sufficient evidence of historicity. However, viewed in light of the genre, purpose, and date of composition of the accounts, the number of manuscripts becomes supportive of an accurate account of events. Remember, the Gospel accounts were written as biographies—as history—no more than 50 years after the events they describe. It would not have been difficult to verify with any number of eyewitnesses if the events were genuinely true, and if they were not confirmed as true, the accounts would have quickly been dismissed as unworthy of being copied, especially unworthy of being copied so many times. Such a high number of original language copies gives credence not only to the purpose of the claims made in the Gospels (to report actual history) but also to the trustworthiness of those claims. All these points of evidence, when considered in conjunction with each other, provide reasonable certainty to the accuracy and reliability of the Gospel accounts—the historical documents that record the life, death, and, yes, resurrection of Jesus.

Integrity of the Documents

In addition to the genre, time frame, and copies of the Gospel accounts, we must also consider the actual content. Shouldn't we be skeptical of its claims since, after all, they're part of a religious text interested in advancing a particular agenda. Wouldn't the authors simply put in there whatever helped their cause—whatever was self-serving? Any careful consideration of the trustworthiness of the biblical texts (particularly of the Gospel accounts) must address these concerns.

We must be careful not to discredit the historical claims of the New Testament simply because they are in the Bible. When these documents were composed, they were written as independent historical documents. They were not canonized as official scripture and put in the context of the full Bible until later. They are products of real people who witnessed real events and independently wrote down real history. Their accounts were scrutinized, validated, copiously copied, and only later became part of what we now know as the Bible. Historically speaking, they stand on their own merit, independent of their role as just a piece of the New Testament canon. Each document deserves a fair shake, so to speak, when being evaluated on the basis of their content and whether or not they are filled with content fabricated to serve an agenda.

When we turn to the content itself, we quickly notice that the authors were far more concerned with accurately reporting the events than they were with spinning their story to support an agenda. The Gospel narratives contain details that cannot be explained by anything other than their historicity. If the author was primarily interested in gaining influence and support, much of the content may have been considered foolish and would have rendered him unsuccessful in his agenda.

Jesus

The first indicator that the authors didn't simply record whatever was necessary to progress their agenda is the content about what Jesus said and did. Many times, Jesus turned to the crowd and, in an effort to whittle down the large numbers following him, said something that was either confusing or offensive—oftentimes both. For instance, he told a group of people that had gathered to hear him teach that if they don't hate their own father and mother, they can't be his disciples.[22] Another time, he told a crowd that unless they "eat the flesh of the Son of Man and drink his blood," they could not be true followers.[23] We can hardly find fault with the response that we see in the following verses: "When many of his disciples heard it, they said, 'This is a hard saying; who can listen to it?'"[24] Of course, all of these teachings of Jesus have deeper meanings and need to be properly interpreted, but we can hardly assume that the Gospel writers would have included such difficult, seemingly unwelcoming language if their goal was to amass a following and if they were willing to fabricate the material in order to do so. Also consider Jesus's behavior that they reported. First, he dines with prostitutes and drunkards while openly and publicly opposing the conservative moral and religious elite. One might suggest, "Ah, but of course the Gospel writers would associate him with such people; it's attractive to the masses." If, then, they were making up such a narrative, it certainly would not include the constant instruction from Jesus to repent and turn from your sin. Certainly, the morally licentious target audience would not appreciate being called sinners and told they must repent of their current lifestyle. Jesus does not play into the hands of the fundamentalists, nor does he placate to the licentious. That is just one example among many pointing to the fact that the accounts of Jesus do not fit any one particular social or political agenda and thus cannot be said to have been created to do so.

The twelve apostles

Another self-defeating aspect of the Gospel narratives is the depiction of Jesus's apostles. If the authors felt they had a license to fabricate information and construct any narrative they wished to support their agenda, we can be assured that the portrait of the apostles would look quite different than the one we have.

Peter, for instance, widely recognized as one of the more prominent if not the most prominent leader of the church after Jesus's ministry concluded, often appears impulsive, ignorant, and, worst of all, disloyal. He repeatedly speaks out of place, he openly criticizes and rebukes

Jesus, and he denies even knowing Jesus three times while Jesus is on trial and suffering prior to his crucifixion.[25]

Peter's portrayal in particular becomes even stronger evidence for the Gospels' integrity when we consider that his own eyewitness testimony was essential to Mark's Gospel account. Mark and Peter traveled together and worked together while recording the events in question. Practically speaking, Peter had an opportunity to shape Mark's account to his advantage, thus shaping the content that other Gospel writers—Matthew and Luke—had to work with as well. If Peter had taken creative license with how he "remembered" the events, would he not set himself up as a figure to be trusted? Or if Mark wanted to support his friend and partner, he could have simply left out Peter's mistakes. At the very least, he would have left out Peter's infamous denials of Jesus. Mark would want to make sure he was portrayed as courageous, intelligent, and resourceful—as worthy of being followed. Yet, the Gospel accounts show a very different (much less favorable) description. The only explanation for such things being included in the story, then, is that they are true. It's clear that for Mark, and for the other authors, historical accuracy took precedence over creating a narrative with a favorable spin on the characters.

It's worth mentioning that when we consider the other disciples, we encounter the same problem. All 12 of the people whom Jesus handpicked to continue his movement repeatedly second-guessed Jesus's ability or simply did not understand what he was plainly saying.[26] Again, the only explanation of such a negative portrait of the closest followers of Jesus is that it's an accurate one.

The fact that the authors were committed solely to reporting the events as they happened makes the rapid growth of Christianity in the first few centuries after Jesus all the more remarkable. It's clear that they weren't trying to trick people into joining their cause. To be sure, if the authors had generated only self-serving content, perhaps an expansive spread of the Christian worldview would make more sense. But such an account of historical fact alone can only mean one thing: the facts about the events were so incredible, so transformative, and so life-changing that there was no need to alter them in any way. Even alongside the seemingly self-defeating content contained in the Gospels, the historical news therein was enough to catalyze a truly astonishing number of converts. That means the news itself would need to be worthy of such a response. News of a resurrection certainly fit the bill.

Paul's Letters

While the Gospel accounts are the primary source of information we have on the person and ministry of Jesus, there are other documents that substantiate the claims that the authors of the Gospels made. The apostle Paul was the most influential missionary and author of the earliest stages of Christianity. He wrote prolifically and traveled across the ancient world, reporting the news of Jesus's death and resurrection. In one of his letters to the church at Corinth, Paul makes a profound claim about the validity of Jesus's resurrection:

> *For I delivered to you as of first importance what I also received: that Christ died for our sins in accordance with the Scriptures, that he was buried, that he was raised on the third day in accordance with the Scriptures, and that he appeared to Cephas, then to the twelve. Then he appeared to more than five hundred brothers at one time, most of whom are still alive, though some have fallen asleep.*[27]

"Then he appeared to more than five hundred brothers at one time, most of whom are still alive"—In order to make such a claim, Paul would have had to be certain that it was verifiable. Essentially, he's saying: "You don't believe me? Go ask the hundreds of people who saw him. They're still alive." Scholars confidently date the writing of this letter to Corinth somewhere between AD 53 and AD 55. That's only 20 years after the resurrection of Jesus. Many people who were alive at the time would have still been alive and would remember the events of Jesus very well.

At this point, it's important to note that the claim of a man coming back from the dead was just as incredulous to a first-century audience as it would be to a modern one. It's easy to assume that the ancients simply didn't understand the laws of nature, but they did. C. S. Lewis humorously notes that the reason Joseph was concerned about Mary's unexpected pregnancy and assumed marital unfaithfulness wasn't because he *didn't* understand the laws of nature but precisely because he *did*.[28] Of course, our grasp of many scientific disciplines has grown tremendously since then, but the ancients very much understood that people who died stayed dead. This means that the claim that a man died and came back to life again would have been as heavily

The Historical Documents

doubted and scrutinized as it would be today. People would have put a lot of effort into validating or disproving such an outlandish claim. Paul understood the difficulty that people would have in taking his claim seriously; he was sympathetic to their doubts. So he engaged their doubts with reason. He understood that the claim of a resurrection is not one that would be easily believed, based on the testimony of one person. Several hundred independent witnesses with no motivation to alter the truth, however, far surpassed the corroboration necessary to substantiate the claim.

Plenty of people were interested in disproving Jesus's resurrection. It was problematic for Jewish and Roman government officials alike, and all they had to do was ask the people to whom Paul referred, prove Paul was lying, and completely undermine his personal credibility and the validity of anything he had written. People would have quickly dismissed him as a fraud. His reputation and writings did not have their credibility undermined, though. Instead, his letters were fervently reproduced and widely circulated.

Let's consider a parallel from modernity. On April 19, 1995, Timothy McVeigh and Terry Nichols set off a truck bomb in Oklahoma City that killed 168 people and injured 680 more. Those who witnessed the event and its aftermath surely will never forget it. It was life-altering. The event was forever imprinted in their minds. If someone wanted to convince someone else that the Oklahoma City bombing didn't happen, it would be a nearly impossible task. Why? Because people saw it. They experienced it. The truthfulness of the event was solidified by the people who witnessed it. Did the person who wrote the history textbook describing the event see it? Perhaps. Perhaps not. Nevertheless, that writer could give an account of the event confidently because more than enough people *did* witness it.

This is the level of confidence Paul has in recounting the resurrection. He invites his doubters to see for themselves. He welcomes them, saying that if he's making this up, they can easily prove him wrong. Yet, as already mentioned, we have more copies of New Testament books, including Paul's letters, than any other classical work. Such a large number of people would not have deemed Paul's letters worthy of transcribing if he had been quickly disproved. Because of the time frame in which Paul's letters were written and because of how easily he could have been dispelled as a fraud, the only logical conclusion is that the claims he made were not only verifiable, but actually verified. That means we either have to presume we are intellectually superior to nearly everyone in the first century or that Jesus did, indeed, come back from the dead.

Conclusion

The reliability and integrity of the Gospel accounts and Paul's letters as historical documents have hopefully been made clear. The genre of the material can be trusted, the time frame in which they were written allows for eyewitness accuracy, and the number of manuscripts shows how significant the documents were to the original readers. Additionally, with regard to the Gospel accounts in particular, the content of the documents is far too self-defeating to allow for the possibility that the authors constructed a narrative to support their purpose. If someone is going to continue doubting the resurrection of Jesus, that person must do so while at least acknowledging that it means ignoring the overwhelming historical trustworthiness of the accounts that report it. Fortunately, though, there is still more to consider. Next, we tighten the scope of the lens and zoom in on a particular part of the historical documents: the resurrection accounts themselves.

Chapter 6

The Resurrection Accounts

Roll away your stone, I'll roll away mine;
Together we can see what we will find.
—*Mumford & Sons*

Though stylistic differences exist between the endings of each of the Gospels, they all conclude in the same way, with an account of Jesus's resurrection. For each of the Gospel writers who were telling about Jesus—who he was and what he came to do—the resurrection was essential. Matthew includes some of Jesus's teachings that aren't found elsewhere, Luke includes a few parables that can only be found in his account, and John's Gospel is certainly unique in many ways. However, they all find common ground at least in one thing: the importance of Jesus's rising from the dead. And if we look closely at those resurrection narratives, we'll find indicators that give an added measure of credibility to their reporting.

Immediately after the time of Jesus, people began positing alternative theories that could explain the consequences of a resurrection without a resurrection actually taking place. We'll address those individually in a later chapter, but a few of them rely on a common premise: the belief that

Jesus rose from the dead didn't exist until much later after his death. They suggest that stories of Jesus's resurrection developed later either as a coping mechanism or as a hoax, and then, after they were absorbed into Christian traditions, they were later added to the Gospel accounts. This allows for the argument that although the Gospels were written within the lifetime of the apostles and the eyewitnesses, the resurrection accounts that conclude each of them were not written until long after and then added by future leaders of the church in order to inspire followers.

Early Composition

The obvious task ahead, then, is to show that the resurrection accounts were not developed later and added to the Gospel accounts. A close examination of them will allow us to do just that. In fact, several aspects of the accounts confirm that not only were they not fabricated and added later, but they were actually verified and being spread significantly *before* the writing of the Gospels, immediately after the event in question.[29]

Helpful discrepancies

Typically, people use discrepancies between complementary narratives as a reason *not* to believe in the truthfulness of the Bible. They are sometimes wrongfully labeled as contradictions.[30] However, if we consider the slight discrepancies between the resurrection accounts (such as the number of women who went to the tomb or who greeted them there), we'll see that these differences don't undermine the validity of the primary event in question; instead, they bolster it.

The Resurrection Accounts 85

Imagine that you are a member of a jury. The prosecutor has just called an eyewitness to the stand who claims to have seen the robbery in question. She tells her account to you and your fellow jurors. After she concludes, another witness takes the stand and gives his account of what happened. You notice subtle differences between the stories: the color of the getaway car (one witness said black, the other said grey) and the time of day (one said 1:30 p.m. and the other said 1:45 p.m.). The differences are not drastic, but they're noticeable. Imagine the same scenario, except this time the two witnesses give perfectly aligned stories. Every detail matches. Not only do they agree on the color of the car, but they each describe it as graphite grey, and without hesitation they both note that the time was 1:37 p.m. You are now understandably suspicious. What are the chances that two independent witnesses, in the midst of a traumatic event, would happen to choose such a precise color choice and both look at the time at the same exact minute and remembered it, despite the chaos around them? You now wonder, did the robbery happen as told? Did it happen at all? Even without legal training, we know from common sense and intuition alone that the first scenario, not only despite the differences but *because* of them, describes more reliable eyewitness testimonies.

The same is true with the resurrection accounts that are included in each Gospel. The slight narrative differences don't harm their reliability; they add to it. They give credence to the fact that a remarkable, significant event occurred, and people began sharing it and recording it as quickly as possible. They didn't have time to polish the details and make sure they aligned with all the other versions, nor were they interested in doing so. They simply wanted to make sure people knew that Jesus had come back from the dead. That's what was important. And so they simply began to tell of the event the best they could because it was such important news. If the Gospel writers or later editors were making up the resurrection even many years after Jesus's death, they would have had plenty of time to corroborate their stories. Instead, we see resurrection accounts that formed before the Gospels were completed as written works.

No Old Testament

One of the other marks of the resurrection accounts that indicate a very early composition is the lack of Old Testament quotations and references. Throughout each of the four Gospels, the authors draw from the Hebrew Bible to show how everything that Jesus did was done in accordance with the scriptures or so the scriptures could be fulfilled. Even when not stated explicitly, a connection between the teachings and works of Jesus and the Old Testament can be found. However, this is not the case with the accounts of Jesus's rising from the dead.

If the authors of the Gospels or later editors were fabricating the resurrection—if they had decided it would be a good way to end the story—then we would expect that they would have linked this event to the Old Testament, as they had done with other significant acts of Jesus throughout their works. Even by the time Paul was writing his letters, he linked the resurrection to the Hebrew scriptures. And remember, he was writing his letters very shortly after Jesus's ministry—within about 20 years. That means that accounts of the resurrection were being spread even earlier than that. When people began telling others about what Jesus had done, they had not yet had time to figure out how it related to their current theological framework. They hadn't yet aligned it with prophecies in their scriptures. They simply began stating the facts of the event. All that was important is that it happened. It wasn't until Paul's writings that early Christians began to figure out how it conformed to what had been promised in the Old Testament.

Jesus's unremarkable description

One of the most surprising—and validating—aspects of the resurrection stories is the appearance of Jesus himself after he rose from the dead. He's described in a manner that is hardly awe-inspiring. In fact, in many ways, it's rather underwhelming. In John's account, Mary Magdalene mistakes Jesus for a gardener at first and then only recognizes him after a second look.[31] In Luke's account, some of the disciples failed to recognize Jesus while walking with him on the way to Emmaus.[32] Such confusion couldn't have happened if Jesus was majestically clothed or if he was shining in splendor and glory, as one might expect him to be had his resurrection been imagined later as a way to inspire followers and garner support. If you were inventing a story of someone conquering death and reigning over the world, would you give him an appearance that could be mistaken for a gardener? Of course not!

Similar to his physical appearance, we find him engaged in surprisingly human activities after his resurrection—eating breakfast, for instance.[33] Had someone fabricated the resurrection in an attempt to prove Jesus's divinity and power, eating breakfast would have hardly been an inspiring choice of behavior. The only explanation for Jesus's unremarkable appearance and actions after his resurrection is that it was true, and people noted it right away.

The women at the tomb

The strongest evidence for the integrity of the resurrection accounts is contained in the sections depicting the discovery of the empty tomb. Every author tells of the empty tomb being discovered and reported by women.

Hopefully, to you and me that detail seems inconsequential. We might say, "Okay, women saw and reported it first. So what?" In our worldview, one's gender has no bearing on his or her ability to witness and report information. No one accepts or dismisses the validity of a claim solely on whether a man or woman makes it. Unfortunately, this was not always the case. Even less than a century ago, women were not seen as qualified to participate in the political system. One can imagine the far greater struggles women faced nearly two millennia ago. One of those struggles that is particularly relevant was that the testimony of a woman was not admissible in court. If someone committed a crime but only a woman (or women) witnessed it, they could not testify, and there was thus no proof of guilt. An event that only a woman witnessed was an event that, in the eyes of the law, might as well have not happened.

Why, then, would every Gospel writer give an account of an empty tomb that was first discovered and reported by women? The only possible reason is that they were committed to historical accuracy above all else. Imagine the conundrum of the authors: fabricate information about the most important event in their narrative to support their claim or report the events the way they actually happened and potentially undermine their credibility, rendering the rest of their work meaningless. Even Jesus's disciples, after being told many times that he would resurrect on the third day, did not believe the women's claims. Luke reported that "these words [speaking of the empty tomb] seemed to them an idle tale, and they [the apostles] did not believe them."[34]

What's more, by the time the resurrection narrative made its way into Paul's letters, the eyewitness testimonies of the women were nowhere to be found. The women had been redacted from the story. Paul knew it would be apologetic suicide to include them. Nevertheless, all four Gospel writers included them. If they or later editors were willing to lie to achieve their goal, the women's eyewitness accounts of the empty tomb would surely have been the first thing to go. Yet all four accounts stay true to history and report that the empty tomb was, in fact, discovered and reported by women. The only explanation is that the event in question actually happened and that people began recounting the event immediately after it occurred.

Conclusion

To say that the resurrection stories emerged later out of a fabricated idea and were then added to the Gospel accounts is to simply neglect the basic tools of historical investigation. There are far too many indicators of a very early formation of the accounts. The Gospel writers and their contemporaries were clearly trying to convince their readers that Jesus was Lord of all—that he was God's true Messiah, sent to save the world. John said:

> *These are written so that you may believe that Jesus is the Christ, the Son of God, and that by believing you may have life in his name.*[35]

If the writers had motivation to alter any part of the Gospel narratives, it would be the accounts of Jesus's resurrection. Everything hinged on whether or not he came back from the dead. If they had time to polish their stories, create convincing arguments, and create the most favorable accounts possible, they would have included things that are absent and removed things that are present. The only reasonable conclusion is that the events were being reported (1) as they happened and (2) before the written Gospels were completed.

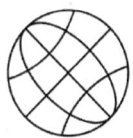

Chapter 7
A Life-Changing Event

I'll never be the same.
—Billie Holiday

In one of the opening songs of the musical *Les Misérables*, one of the protagonists, Jean Valjean, sings a soliloquy in response to the kindness and grace of a local clergyman. Upon being released from prison after serving nearly 20 years, Valjean steals some valuables from the bishop's home. He is caught red-handed, and the bishop could have easily had Valjean locked back up for a long time. Instead of turning him in, though, the man sets Valjean free and lets him keep what he stole to use to begin a new, honest life. In a moment, Valjean experiences more hope than he had previously thought possible. His soliloquy reveals his thought process as he's working through this life-altering event, and it ends with a triumphant declaration of a new beginning: "I'll escape now from that world, / From the world of Jean Valjean; / Jean Valjean is nothing now / Another story must begin!"[36]

The kindness of the bishop shatters his paradigm. He experienced unimaginable hope and is moved to throw away his old self and take on a new purpose in life. He commits himself to serving others, seeking justice, and living a life of integrity. His life now had two distinct chapters—two stories, as he says—each lived by wholly different people. And in the middle of these two chapters lies a single experience.

Experiences change people. You can most likely pinpoint several life-changing moments that you've experienced, and perhaps there's even one that stands out above the rest. And when thinking back through such experiences, you'll notice that the more remarkable the event is, the more drastic the change that follows. So when we examine an event as astonishing as a resurrection and the hope that it provides, we expect to see equally astonishing changes in the people who experienced it. And that's exactly what we find.

James, the Brother of Jesus

We've mentioned James before. He was the brother of Jesus. The two grew up in the same house—they ate dinner together, were tucked in at night in the same house, and went to school together. Many feel they have a sibling that is perfect in their parents' eyes and is the favorite. I assure you, James could empathize. Imagine, though, what James's response was when Jesus began to make claims that he was the Son of God and the Messiah—the promised savior of the world! Imagine that your sibling all of a sudden began making claims of authority over the entire cosmos. What would your response be if he told you he was God himself in the flesh? We would expect James to respond the same way we would—with doubt. And we find evidence of James's skepticism in John's Gospel account:

> *Now the Jews' Feast of Booths was at hand. So his brothers said to him, "Leave here and go to Judea, that your disciples also may see the works you are doing. For no one works in secret if he seeks to be known openly. If you do these things, show yourself to the world."* **For not even his brothers believed in him** (emphasis added). [37]

What, then, could have caused someone so skeptical to become a figure of great influence in the early church? How could James have gone from doubtful brother to loyal follower and supporter—even to the point of being martyred? He had a significant experience that produced a significant change.

After Jesus's resurrection, James became an adamant supporter of Jesus's message and mission. We know from the works of Josephus, an ancient historian, that James was stoned to death because of his faith in Jesus—faith in his own brother. And Eusibius, another ancient historian, gives us this record:

> They [the Scribes and Pharisees] came . . . to James, and said: "We entreat thee, restrain the people: for they have gone astray in their opinions about Jesus, as if he were the Christ [the Messiah]. . . . For we all listen to thy persuasion; since we, as well as all the people, bear thee testimony that thou art just, and showest partiality to none. Do thou, therefore, persuade the people not to entertain

erroneous opinions concerning Jesus: for all the people, and we also, listen to thy persuasion?"[38]

The religious leaders—the ones trying to quell the testimonies of a divine (risen) Jesus—said that James was a trustworthy and just man that people will listen to. They hoped that his levelheadedness would persuade people to abandon the fanciful notions of Jesus's divinity. It was certainly much to their chagrin that James's response was, "Christ himself sitteth in heaven, at the right hand of the Great Power, and shall come on the clouds of heaven."[39]

Their plan backfired. They assumed they could use James's testimony to undermine the public news of Jesus's resurrection, but James, utterly convinced of his brother's divinity and authority, only reinforced what the public was beginning to believe: that Jesus is the Son of God, that he was raised from the dead, and that he is the Messiah—God's savior to the world. The scribes and Pharisees quickly realized their error, and they stoned James to death. Only an event as remarkable as a resurrection could turn a hardened skeptic into someone willing to die for the chance to proclaim the truth that he had come to believe about his brother.

The Apostle Paul

Another prominent figure whose life is a testimony to Jesus's resurrection is Paul. Next to Jesus, Paul is arguably the most influential figure in the church's history. Of all of Jesus's followers, in any time period, Paul's contributions—his missionary journeys and epistles—are the most significant. It would surprise someone unfamiliar

A Life-Changing Event

with Paul to learn, then, that he lived the majority of his life as a zealous Jewish leader, hell-bent on destroying the Christian message and anyone who believed it. What could convince a man who was utterly opposed to Jesus to suddenly devote his entire life to making sure as many people knew about Jesus as possible? Significant events produce significant change. Here is what Paul wrote about his own conversion:

> *For I delivered to you as of first importance what I also received: that Christ died for our sins in accordance with the Scriptures, that he was buried, that he was raised on the third day in accordance with the Scriptures, and that he appeared to Cephas, then to the twelve. Then he appeared to more than five hundred brothers at one time, most of whom are still alive, though some have fallen asleep. Then he appeared to James, then to all the Apostles. Last of all, as to one untimely born, he appeared also to me. For I am the least of the apostles, unworthy to be called an apostle, because I persecuted the church of God. But by the grace of God I am what I am, and his grace toward me was not in vain.*[40]

We discussed these words in 1 Corinthians 15 before in reference to Paul's invitation to corroborate the claim of Jesus's resurrection. But Paul continued, claiming that he was "unworthy to be called an apostle." Why? Because he "persecuted the church of God." What could reverse his zeal against Jesus's mission? Paul told us, "Last of all he appeared also to me." There are not many things that could cause a worldview reversal as drastically as Paul's. Encountering someone who had come back from the dead, though, certainly could.

The Twelve Apostles

We now turn our consideration to a whole group: Jesus's apostles. The Gospel narratives contain many instances of the apostles' fear, apprehension, and lack of commitment. They repeatedly second-guessed Jesus when he spoke of his purpose and mission, they doubted Jesus's ability to heal and protect, and they even fell asleep when Jesus asked them to be on guard while he prayed the night before he was crucified.[41] That's not the group of men whom one would naturally recruit to boldly and effectively carry on one's mission. During their time with Jesus, their displays of doubt and fear were far more noticeable than their confidence and valor.

How, then, are we to explain how every one of these men were unwavering in their commitments to the mission and message of Jesus, even in most cases to the point of excruciating death? What could transform a group from disloyal to dedicated—from fearful tradesmen to courageous martyrs? What could lead someone like Peter from denying any affiliation with Jesus to facing his own crucifixion with grace and poise? No matter how unfortunate any of their fates were, they couldn't neglect the fact that the tomb of their Lord was empty.

This is perhaps one of the most relevant times to apply the importance of walking the walk over simply talking the talk. It is feasible that with the proper rhetoric, people could tickle the ears of the masses enough to convince them of something, even if they do not themselves believe it. As we know, though, actions speak louder than words. And few actions speak louder than laying down one's life for a cause, something that nearly every apostle did.

The Early Christians

Second-century church father Tertullian famously wrote that "the blood of the martyrs is the seed of the church."[42] He was referring to the phenomenon of the rapid spread of Christianity in the earliest years of the church, despite rampant persecution. Under emperors such as Nero and Domitian, the Roman government practiced systematic, widespread persecution of those who called themselves Christians. Anyone claiming Jesus as their divine Lord could be subject to public humiliation, brutal torture, and even execution. After all, Caesar was lord, not Jesus. To profess faith in Jesus was to declare oneself an enemy of the Roman state, inviting severe consequences. Why, then, did so many do just that? Why was it that the more the Romans tortured and killed Christians, the more converts the Christian worldview gained? Because if you believe that someone came back from the dead, securing that same hope for you, then death is no longer something to fear. And when others see your fearlessness in the face of death, it's something they're going to be interested in learning about.

Like the apostles, many in the early church paid much more than lip service to their newfound hope. They did more than simply *say* they could face pain, suffering, and death with hope and joy. They *showed* it. They endured some of the most gruesome, painful deaths imaginable. They were thrown to the lions and burned alive on crosses to light up the roads at night. And yet, time after time, the onlooking Romans were stunned by the confidence, poise, and hope with which the Christians faced their fates.

For the early Christians, a secure hope was something they needed on a daily basis. In fact, in the earliest stages of the church, the anchor, not the cross, was the symbol of choice. After all, the cross was still an active form of execution, one that many of them found themselves and their loved ones all too familiar with. The anchor reminded them that their hope was secure and unwavering. In the face of their brutal persecution, they had Jesus, their anchor, to ground them. And because of this concrete source of assurance and hope, they faced the horrors of persecution with songs of praise both in their hearts and on their lips. Can you imagine witnessing a Christian family sing hymns together seconds before their certain death? Only a real hope—a provable hope—could provide that kind of confidence.

Conclusion

The resurrection of Jesus flipped the lives of many people upside down. Those who were skeptics became believers, those who were actively working against Jesus joined his mission, and those who had everything to lose risked it all to place their hope in him. Again, a skilled deceiver might be able to fool a small group of gullible, unintelligent people into a scheme. But what would it take to convince your brother that you are divine? What would it take to turn a highly educated man, who wanted nothing more than to kill your followers and stop your mission, into your greatest ambassador? What would it take to convince those who knew you best—who knew every intimate detail of your life—to become martyrs for your cause? What would it take to convince a sweeping mass of people that

A Life-Changing Event

they don't need to worry about protecting their property, their rights, or their lives because they are assured an eternal reward? Remarkable events produce remarkable change. In some ways, these accounts of changed lives are the most convincing evidence for the resurrection because they're the most relatable. To be sure, the historical documents and philosophical arguments are necessary to consider, but even if we set those to the side for a moment, we can still ask, "What would need to occur—what would I need to be convinced of—to completely undo my current priorities and commit everything I have, even my own life, to someone as my Lord and my hope?" Or perhaps we could ask, "How sure would I have to be before I'd be willing to sacrifice my social status, my possessions, and even my life for the sake of putting my faith in someone?" These were real people who decided to follow Jesus at all costs. Jesus's friends and enemies alike witnessed something significant enough to convince them of his divinity and lordship. What would it take for you to do the same?

Chapter 8
Alternative Theories

*When you have eliminated the impossible,
whatever remains, however improbable,
must be the truth.*

—*Sherlock Holmes*

By this point, it's clear that belief in Jesus's resurrection changed the landscape of history. Even skeptics of his resurrection must admit that the tomb of Jesus was at the very least *believed* to be empty. The rapid spread of Christianity and its central message in the first century confirms that. But what if the whole thing was a hoax? What we cannot argue with is whether or not the apostles and early Christians diligently communicated their belief in Jesus's literal resurrection. Many do argue, though, that the apostles and early Christians were either gravely mistaken or intentionally deceptive about this incredible news.

Of course, this counterargument is largely rooted in an *a priori* commitment against supernatural occurrences (something we covered already). Nevertheless, if we are to faithfully consider the possibility of the resurrection of Jesus, we must also consider the alternatives—the other possible ways the apostles and the early Christians could have become convinced of Jesus's victory over death.

We can begin by saying we need two things to have a convincing resurrection account: an empty tomb and a risen, renewed, living Jesus. If you just have an empty tomb, it only proves the body isn't there. If you only have an appearance of Jesus, then it could be a hallucination or some sort of spiritual vision, and his body could still be in the tomb. So because both of these factors are necessary to convince people of a true resurrection, both must be adequately addressed by each alternative theory.

The Swoon Theory

All the other theories that follow this one assume that Jesus was actually killed during his crucifixion. This one, however, does not. The swoon theory suggests that Jesus was not entirely dead at the time he was taken off the cross but was, instead, *nearly* dead (or, as Miracle Max in *The Princess Bride* would say, "mostly dead"). In other words, Jesus was so badly marred that he appeared to have been successfully executed. He was then buried in a coma-like state, and after a few days he managed to wake up and make his way out of the tomb.

The issues with this theory are several. First, we must consider the likelihood of a person surviving a Roman crucifixion. The Romans widely implemented crucifixion as a means of public execution. Although it was a long, excruciating process, the goal was not merely torture; it was meant to be lethal. The efficacy of crucifixion alone along with the gruesome beatings that Jesus received prior to his execution ensure that the only outcome Jesus was going

Alternative Theories 103

to face was death. A medical study from the *Journal of the American Medical Association* gives us relevant information:

> Jesus of Nazareth underwent Jewish and Roman trials, was flogged, and was sentenced to death by crucifixion. The scourging produced deep stripelike lacerations and appreciable blood loss, and it probably set the stage for hypovolemic shock, as evidenced by the fact that Jesus was too weakened to carry the crossbar (patibulum) to Golgotha. At the site of crucifixion, his wrists were nailed to the patibulum and, after the patibulum was lifted onto the upright post (stipes), his feet were nailed to the stipes. The major pathophysiologic effect of crucifixion was an interference with normal respirations. Accordingly, death resulted primarily from hypovolemic shock and exhaustion asphyxia. Jesus' death was ensured by the thrust of a soldier's spear into his side. Modern medical interpretation of the historical evidence indicates that Jesus was dead when taken down from the cross.[43]

Jesus could not have survived his crucifixion. However, for the sake of argument, let's assume that he did—that he wasn't fully dead and was put in the tomb bloodied and battered, clinging to life. The idea that he managed to crawl out some days later and convince his followers that he had resurrected is even more difficult to accept.

Let's consider how a man marred nearly beyond recognition and nearly dead could get out of a tomb that was covered with a large stone and guarded by a Roman military post. How does he nurse his wounds while he is in a coma? How does he recover his strength? How, then, does he push a large stone to the side and subdue or avoid the guards charged with ensuring the security of the tomb? It's clear that if Jesus were nearly dead enough to fool the Roman soldiers who crucified him (who, by the way, would have faced execution if they had failed to successfully kill a condemned prisoner)[44] and nearly dead enough to have been prepared for burial and buried without anyone noticing (after his friends and family had closely handled his body), then he was also nearly dead enough to be completely incapable of making it out of his grave.

However, again, for the sake of argument, let's grant that Jesus somehow survived the crucifixion and then somehow, someway made it out of the tomb and past the military post. We're left with still the most convincing argument against this theory. How does a man who does all of the above instill in his followers the belief that he had conquered death, and in so doing, convince them that they, too, will be victorious over death because of their hope in him?

The followers of Jesus did not commit their lives to the spread of Jesus's message and ultimately die for the cause because they believed Jesus managed to simply not die. They had to have been convinced that death itself was beatable, not just marginally escapable. D. F. Strauss, someone who nevertheless still denied the resurrection, recognized that this theory ought to be rejected:

> It is impossible that a being who had stolen half-dead out of the sepulcher, who crept about weak and ill,

wanting medical treatment, who required bandaging, strengthening, and indulgence, and who still at last yielded to his sufferings, could have given to the disciples the impression that he was a Conqueror over death and the grave, the Prince of Life, an impression which lay at the bottom of their future ministry.[45]

So we can be reasonably certain (1) that Jesus actually died as a result of his crucifixion, (2) that if he somehow did not die, he could not have escaped the tomb in the nearly dead, comatose state he was in, and (3) that if he somehow survived the crucifixion and somehow made his way out of the tomb, he would not have been able to begin a widespread movement predicated on the foundational belief that he had defeated death and guaranteed that his followers could do the same. For all of these reasons, the swoon theory fails to adequately serve as a substitute for an actual resurrection.

The Stolen Body Theory

Since the suggestion that Jesus did not die and only swooned into a half-dead, half-alive state is a nearly impossible case to make, most of the other alternatives to a resurrection that have been posited center on the idea that Jesus really was dead when he was buried. From there, they suggest that in some way or another his followers either became convinced of a resurrection or fabricated the narrative themselves.

The stolen body theory is precisely what it sounds like. Essentially, it says the apostles pulled off the most elaborate, successful scheme in history: they stole the body of Jesus and managed to convince everyone that he had resurrected. There are several problems with this theory, though, not least being the apostles' ability to accomplish this ruse given the opposition they would have needed to overcome. The theft of Jesus's body was something that the Jewish leaders were wary of and prepared for. In Matthew's account, we read this:

> *The next day, . . . the chief priests and the Pharisees gathered before Pilate and said, "Sir, we remember how that impostor said, while he was still alive, 'After three days I will rise.' Therefore order the tomb to be made secure until the third day, lest his disciples go and steal him away and tell the people, 'He has risen from the dead,' and the last fraud will be worse than the first." Pilate said to them, "You have a guard of soldiers. Go, make it as secure as you can." So they went and made the tomb secure by sealing the stone and setting a guard.* [46]

This means we must assume that Jesus's disciples, a group of tradesmen, were able to outwit and overpower a station of Roman soldiers. We repeatedly receive glimpses into the apostles' competency throughout the Gospel accounts, and together they hardly give the impression that they would have been capable of such a feat. Let's say, for the sake of argument, though, that they were able to pull of this stunt. We then must consider their ability to maintain their story and sufficiently hide any evidence of their theft.

You can ask yourself to what lengths you would be willing to go in order to keep that kind of secret from a highly-trained force determined to prove you're lying. Both the Jewish and the Roman authorities had one chance at maintaining order and control: prove the apostles had duped everyone. Yet not one apostle—not one follower of Jesus—gave in and turned over a body. Again, we know what courage—or, lack of courage—the apostles possessed prior to the resurrection. If they didn't hand over a body, it wasn't because they remained steadfast in their lie, it was because they didn't have a body to hand over.

Aside from the apostles' ability to accomplish this task, we must also consider their motivation to do so. Nearly all of the apostles died a martyr's death after committing their lives to spreading the news of Jesus's divinity and lordship. They did not stand to gain worldly influence or wealth; the only things that were promised to them because of their commitment to the news of Jesus's resurrection were torture and execution. It would be unreasonable to assume each apostle individually and independently sacrificed everything, including their lives, for something they knew all along to be a scam. J. Warner Wallace, a cold-case homicide detective and former atheist, sums up the impossibility of the apostles' so-called hoax like this:

> I am hesitant to embrace any theory that requires the conspiratorial effort of a large number of people over a significant period of time when they personally gain little or nothing by their effort. This theory requires us to believe that the Apostles were transformed and emboldened not by the miraculous appearance of the resurrected Jesus but by elaborate lies created without any benefit to those who were perpetuating the hoax.[47]

When faced with the realization that the apostles both could not and would not have stolen the body and fabricated a resurrection narrative, some have suggested that it was, in fact, the Jewish authorities and leaders who stole the body preemptively in order to prevent the apostles from being able to do so. Presumably, the Jewish authorities were fearful that the followers of Jesus were planning to steal the body and give the illusion of a resurrection, and so they acted first, robbing any followers of their chance.

While the question of motive is easily answered, this theory is betrayed by a glaring logical inconsistency. If the Jewish leaders at the time were set against Jesus and his followers, not wanting to lose their influence and status, all they would have had to do to stop the spread of Christianity once and for all was produce the body of Jesus for people to see. If they had stolen the body, proving that Jesus didn't resurrect, that would have been easy. They would have told everyone, "See? He's just a man!" If they had done that, the Christian worldview would have been dead on arrival.

Given all this, it's clear that this theory does not serve as a legitimate alternative to a resurrection. For one, the likelihood of such a conspiracy being pulled off is nearly non-existent. And as we mentioned earlier, two things are necessary to confirm a resurrection: an empty tomb and visible confirmation of a risen person. That means that alternative theories must provide an explanation for each of these. While this theory could potentially provide an explanation for the empty tomb, however unlikely it may be, it fails to account for the eyewitness accounts of Jesus's appearances to hundreds upon hundreds of people. There are other alternatives to consider, though.

Alternative Theories

The Wrong Tomb Theory

While the wrong tomb theory is almost not worth mentioning, it has been suggested as an alternative to a resurrection, so we'll address it. The proposition is that the followers of Jesus did, in fact, find an empty tomb, but it simply wasn't the tomb of Jesus. In other words, they went to the wrong tomb.

Two primary problems arise when considering the possibility of this theory. The first is the notability of Jesus's tomb. Although we're not entirely sure what it looked like, we do know a few details about it. We know that the tomb belonged to a man named Joseph of Arimathea, a prominent member of the Sanhedrin, the council of Jewish religious leaders. He was a wealthy man, and he personally requested to oversee the burial of Jesus, providing a tomb in a garden in which no one had been laid.[48] We also know, from Mark's account, that both Mary Magdalene and Mary, the mother of Jesus, were present at the burial.[49] And finally, as already mentioned, the Roman governor, Pontius Pilate, placed centurions at the tomb as guards. All of these factors make Jesus's tomb significantly more notable than simply one tomb among many.

We cannot reasonably say that every one of his followers independently went to a tomb that was not his, particularly because, again, Mary Magdalene and Mary, Jesus's mother, both witnessed his burial at this particularly unique tomb. If one of Jesus's disciples went to the wrong tomb and reported the news of it being empty to the rest of Jesus's family, friends, and followers, it would not take long before several of them would simply inform him of his mistake.

Again, the likelihood of this theory serving as a legitimate alternative is too low to seriously consider it.

Finally, as we've repeatedly stated, an empty tomb is not the only criterion necessary for a believable resurrection story. Plenty of tombs could be empty. But this theory also fails to account for the eyewitness confirmation of Jesus's appearance that repeatedly were corroborated, so we can reasonably say this theory does not suffice.

The Hallucination Theory

While the above theories have attempted to address the emptiness (or perceived emptiness) of Jesus's tomb, the so-called hallucination theory aims to explain the physical appearances of a risen Jesus to the eyewitnesses who saw him. As the name suggests, the assumption is that anyone who saw a living Jesus after his death was hallucinating. Proponents of this theory suggest that the loss of Jesus was so stressful and the suffering was so real that his followers, friends, and family all imagined he was alive again and "saw" his appearance in their presence.

While it is reasonable to assume that any one member of Jesus's inner circle could have hallucinated and "seen" his presence (this has been known to happen in rare cases of someone losing a loved one), it is not reasonable to imagine that this could have explained his appearance to hundreds of people independently. Jesus appeared to many individuals in many settings over several weeks. Again, one or maybe even a few hallucinations or instances of feeling his presence could be entertained, but the idea that hundreds of people all happened to experience the same phenomenon in different areas at different times cannot be taken seriously.[50]

And of course, if any person had imagined they saw a risen Jesus, the rest of his family and friends obviously would have quickly dispelled the notion. Imagine if someone in your family was trying to convince others that he or she had seen someone you had previously lost and that person was actually back from the dead. Everyone else who knew that person would simply not go along with it, much less buy into the idea.

Finally, we return to the two criteria necessary for a convincing resurrection. While this theory attempts to provide an explanation for the appearances of Jesus (albeit an inadequate one), it does not address the matter of the empty tomb. Even if all the appearances were somehow hallucinations, a quick display of Jesus's body would have reversed any momentum that a resurrection narrative could have gained. While it is creative, this theory is not a valid alternative.

The Myth Theory

The myth theory is unique among the possible alternatives since it suggests that Jesus's earliest followers didn't actually believe he rose from the dead and Christians later convinced themselves that he had. In other words, there was no attempt at falsifying a resurrection; it was simply conjured up many years later and absorbed into the Christian faith.

Again, we encounter problems, not least being that the concept of a bodily resurrection was not a prominent consideration in ancient Jewish thought. While they would have believed in a future resurrection at the Day of Judgment, a single resurrection in this sense was not something that his followers would have been expecting. While this doesn't necessarily mean someone could not have invented the idea, it does mean that it would not have gained sufficient traction. What would the response have been when the first person to conjure up the idea proposed it to his or her peers? What would you say to someone who suggested that someone rose from the dead without any existing expectation or, better yet, without any proof? What's more, not only would everyone have to somehow be convinced of a seemingly farfetched idea, but they would have to be convinced enough to give up their rights, their safety, and even their lives.

Second, and more concretely, we know this theory cannot be considered because of the conclusion we were able to draw in the previous chapter. We know that the accounts of the resurrection were formed and circulated immediately after the event. People began to believe that Jesus rose from the dead very early—earlier than the writing of the Gospels and Paul's letters. And from our conclusions in Chapter 5, we know these beliefs were already being widely recorded within the life span of Jesus's followers and other eyewitnesses. If people were not expecting a resurrection but immediately began spreading the news of one, the only explanation is that people had become convinced because of concrete evidence.

Conclusion

Philip Schaff, a prominent 19th-century historian, once said:

> Historical questions are not like mathematical problems. No argument in favor of the resurrection

will avail with those critics who start with the philosophical assumption that miracles are impossible, and still less with those who deny not only the resurrection of the body, but even the immortality of the soul. But facts are stubborn, and if a critical hypothesis can be proven to be psychologically and historically impossible and unreasonable, the result is fatal to the philosophy which underlies the critical hypothesis. It is not the business of the historian to construct a history from preconceived notions and to adjust it to his own liking, but to *reproduce it from the best evidence and to let it speak for itself* (emphasis added).[51]

When we consider the evidence alone, it leaves only one sensible explanation: that Jesus actually died, was actually buried, and was actually raised from the dead. A true resurrection is the only narrative that adequately accounts for both the emptiness of Jesus's tomb and the physical appearances to eyewitnesses in the weeks following his death. It's also the only narrative that accounts for many other things already discussed—the written documents, the circulating oral traditions, and the changed lives of Jesus's followers.

As Schaff said, to impose preconceived notions onto the evidence in an effort to avoid a particular conclusion is both a logical fallacy and poor historical scholarship. If we commit to exercising intellectual integrity, we must not bring our prejudices against a particular possibility that only leaves us entertaining alternatives whose shortcomings and logical inconsistencies are readily apparent.

Cognitive dissonance

Cognitive dissonance is the state of having inconsistent thoughts, beliefs, or attitudes. It's the tension in our minds that is created when we feel like we know two incompatible pieces of information to both be true. It is my experience that discussing the historical evidence for the resurrection of Jesus often creates cognitive dissonance in people's minds. On the one hand, they are certain that someone could not have literally risen from the dead. On the other hand, all of the objective evidence points to someone having done just that. What happens, then, in their minds, is that an unstoppable force (historical facts) meets an immovable object (the impossibility of a supernatural event). Of course, one of them has to give way to the other. The problem is, as we've said before, the immoveable object only appears to be immovable.

When we consider the possibility of a resurrection, what objective evidence is there that it couldn't happen? What can we point to and say with clarity and assurance, "This proves someone could not have come back from the dead." The answer, of course, is nothing. Both scientifically and philosophically, there is no way to disprove the possibility of a resurrection.

In other words, to reject the historical evidence of Jesus's resurrection because we simply know it could not have happened is more than irresponsible historical research; it's irresponsible reasoning. The reasons why some people reject any supernatural presence in the universe were addressed in earlier chapters, but it's worth repeating: it takes a lot more faith to reconcile the facts with a strictly materialistic worldview than it does to accept one that allows for the supernatural.

Alternative Theories

With that, we conclude this historical evidence section of the book. We now move on to the third and final section in which we will address this question: "So what?" As we've said, the resurrection changes everything. But how so? What does it mean, practically, for you and for me if Jesus rose from the dead? And how do we approach such life-changing implications? These are the questions we will address as we close.

PART III
THE INVITATION

Chapter 9
From Head to Heart

I believe; help my unbelief!
—Mark 9:24

Jonathan Edwards was a Puritan preacher and writer who lived during the first half of the 18th century. He was so influential that high school English classrooms still sample his sermons and writings in their curricula. One of his most important contributions to the fields of theology and philosophy was his work on the relationship between knowledge and affections—the connection between the head and the heart. Here's an excerpt from one of his sermons on the matter:

> There is a twofold understanding or knowledge of good that God has made the mind of man capable of. The first, that which is merely speculative or notional. . . . And the other is that which consists in the sense of the heart. . . . In the former is exercised merely the speculative faculty. . . . In the latter the will, or inclination . . . are mainly concerned.

> There is a difference between having a rational judgment that honey is sweet, and having a sense of its sweetness. A man may have the former, that knows not how honey tastes; but a man can't have the latter, unless he has an idea of the taste of honey in his mind. So there is a difference between believing that a person is beautiful, and having a sense of his beauty. The former may be obtained by hearsay, but the latter only by seeing the countenance. There is a wide difference between mere speculative, rational judging anything to be excellent, and having a sense of its sweetness, and beauty. The former rests only in the head, speculation only is concerned in it; but the heart is concerned in the latter.[52]

What Edwards is saying is that it is one thing to rationally accept a piece of information, but it is something wholly different to believe that information in such a way that it actually alters your affections—that it actually affects you. It's the difference between looking at a sunset, which may include noticing its colors and patterns, and beholding a sunset and being moved by its splendor.

As we move into the final portion of this book, my hope is to move the discussion from simply looking at the resurrection to beholding it—to move the discussion from the head to the heart. If Edwards is right, then mere cognitive recognition of a fact is not sufficient to know it in the truest sense. So assuming the book so far has been persuasive regarding the resurrection's truthfulness, I now want to persuade you as to why it matters. If Jesus did, in fact, rise from the dead, why should that affect not just your understanding of the world but also the way you live in it and the hope you have for it? In other words, everything so far has been aimed at presenting the resurrection of Jesus to your head. Now my hope is that it would be pressed into your heart.

An Honest Evaluation

The first step in seeing how Jesus's resurrection informs our worldview is taking stock of that worldview and the reasons for it. I've always had an immense amount of admiration for people who speak about their worldviews consistently and honestly, even if I disagree with them strongly or if their views come across as shocking. It is far easier to respect people who disagree with you for thoughtful, consistent reasons than people who agree with you for unthoughtful, inconsistent ones. One of the people who best embodied this consistency was Aldous Huxley. Here's what he said about the Christian worldview and his rejection of it:

> I had motives for not wanting the world to have a meaning; and consequently assumed that it had none, and was able without any difficulty to find satisfying reasons for this assumption. The philosopher who finds no meaning in the world is not concerned exclusively with a problem in pure metaphysics. He is also concerned to prove that there is no valid reason why he personally should not do as he wants to do. For myself, as no doubt for most of my friends, the philosophy of meaninglessness was essentially an instrument of liberation from a certain

system of morality. We objected to the morality because it interfered with our sexual freedom. The supporters of this system claimed that it embodied the meaning—the Christian meaning, they insisted—of the world. There was one admirably simple method of confuting these people and justifying ourselves in our erotic revolt: we would deny that the world had any meaning whatever.[53]

Perhaps it's untactful, but it's also remarkably honest. To paraphrase Huxley, he essentially admitted, "I didn't approach the meaning of life from the standpoint of facts and objective knowledge; I did so based on how I wanted to live my life." In other words, and allow me to paraphrase, he believed "Whatever worldview supported what I wanted to do and who I wanted to be was the worldview I would adopt." Not only that, but he also was upfront about his ability to "find satisfying reasons for this assumption."

That is why asking the question, "What do I believe?" isn't sufficient on its own. It's only part of the process. We must also be sure to ask, "*Why* do I believe what I believe? What motives lie beneath my worldview?" Are our beliefs birthed from objective, rational thinking? Or have they been molded by other motives—other desires? I certainly do not mean that everyone who denies the resurrection of Jesus has reasons akin to Huxley's. I am simply suggesting that a careful, reflective evaluation of the *why* behind such a denial is a task whose importance cannot be overstated. There is no event in history worthier of an objective, honest approach.

Considering the Implications

As part of our honest assessment of our heart's posture toward the resurrection of Jesus, we must consider the implications of such an event. Obviously, the significance of a literal resurrection cannot be overstated, but we must also identify what such an event means for our world and how we view it. In so doing, we will be better able to parse through those things that may stand in the way of accepting the truthfulness of the resurrection.

1. If Jesus rose from the dead, he is divine.

We covered this in the book's earlier chapters, but it bears repeating, primarily because it necessarily precedes all of the other implications we are about to discuss. There isn't much else that needs to be said, because the logical connection is quite straightforward. If Jesus possessed the ability to rise from the dead, then he clearly wasn't merely a human in the same sense that you and I are. He was mortal in the sense that he could die, but he was not mortal in the sense that he was subject to death. Not only does Jesus's resurrection affirm the presence of a divine, supernatural existence in the universe, but it also identifies Jesus as the embodiment of it.

Jesus's divinity may not be a roadblock in and of itself, but as a premise, it does lead to several other logical conclusions that may be more difficult to accept.

2. If Jesus rose from the dead, all doubts, questions, and objections regarding Christianity have an answer.

The historical truthfulness of Jesus's resurrection is not always—perhaps even not usually—the primary concern when assessing the Christian worldview. Often, other matters take precedence in both our reasoning and our emotions. These other matters, whether doubts, objections, or inquisitions, should certainly not be dismissed as unimportant. We shouldn't shy away from wrestling with them. Tim Keller addressed the issue of doubting and questioning with this:

> A faith without some doubts is like a human body without any antibodies in it. People who blithely go through life too busy or indifferent to ask hard questions about why they believe as they do will find themselves defenseless against either the experience of tragedy or the probing questions of a smart skeptic. A person's faith can collapse almost overnight if she has failed over the years to listen patiently to her own doubts, which should only be discarded after long reflection. Believers should acknowledge and wrestle with doubts—not only their own but their friends' and neighbors'. It is no longer sufficient to hold beliefs just because you inherited them. Only if you struggle long and hard with objections to your faith will you be able to provide grounds for your beliefs to skeptics, including yourself, that are plausible rather than ridiculous or offensive.[54]

It's a shame that within Christian circles, wrestling with matters of worldview and thinking critically about one's doubts is often seen as weakness. If you grew up in a Christian home, whether you still consider yourself a Christian or not, you probably heard at some point along the way something to the effect of "Just believe." Maybe you've inquired of other Christians with well meaning, honest objections and doubts regarding the Christian worldview, and the answers you receive are subjective platitudes about just having faith even if something doesn't make sense. Or maybe you are a Christian who has been afraid to engage with your own doubts because there's a lingering sense of fear that they could be true. Maybe you were never given any actual reasons why you should be a follower of Jesus. You were just told, perhaps by a parent, that "this is what we believe." But what if it was simply emotionalism all along? Wouldn't it be easier to ignore the doubts and pretend everything will work itself out? Ignorance is bliss, after all. Whatever the case, and whatever the doubt, we need to think critically about it and be comfortable approaching it with objectivity and clarity. The resurrection of Jesus allows us to do just that.

Of course, constraints of time and space don't allow for a robust handling of every topic that could be categorized under this heading, but what I do hope to offer is an approach—an approach that we can (and should) employ when thinking through other issues that hinder the acceptance of Christianity. We'll start, though, with the most common objection.

With all the evil in the world, if there is a God, how can he be both benevolent and sovereign?

The problem of evil has long been a central dilemma in the matter of God's existence and nature. It is often posed as this: "Because evil exists in the world, if God is all-loving, then he is not all-powerful; if he is all-powerful, then he is not all-loving."

Answers to this problem of evil are called theodicies. Most theodicies begin with the relationship between God's sovereignty and the responsibility, moral agency, and free will that God grants to humankind. It is actually possible to reconcile this tension in a variety of ways, but one way to get a more concrete look at this mysterious relationship between divine providence and human influence is to look to the person of Jesus—his character, his teachings, and his revelation to us. Jesus claimed to be fully united with God in nature and will. "I and the Father are one,"[55] he said. Paul describes the relationship between Jesus and God this way: "He is the image of the invisible God" and "in him [Jesus] all the fullness of God was pleased to dwell."[56] When we look at the words and deeds of Jesus, we are peering directly into the heart of God. So what was Jesus's posture toward evil in the world? A good place to start is Jesus's lament over the city of Jerusalem recorded in Matthew's Gospel:

> *O Jerusalem, Jerusalem, the city that kills the prophets and stones those who are sent to it! How often would I have gathered your children together as a hen gathers her brood under her wings, and you were not willing!* [57]

Jesus is expressing sadness over the people's pattern of wickedness. What's more, his distress is compounded by the fact that he wants the people to turn from evil and turn to him to find true meaning and purpose in life. And what does he say? "You were not willing!" The same Jesus that can calm storms, turn water into wine, and give sight to the blind tells us that people's evil deeds are due to their own desires and lack of willingness to pursue goodness. We're thus able to understand that Jesus can love these people and desire for them to cease doing evil. But then this brings us to the matter of why God allows evil in the world. It's true that evil originates from the hearts of men, not from the hand of God. In allowing free will and moral agency, God also allows for the possibility of rebellion, which means he allows for humankind to choose to commit all kinds of atrocious acts. If we know that God can intervene in the affairs of the world whenever and however he chooses, then how are we to understand why he prevents certain things and allows others? How can he allow certain tragedies and still be classified as good or benevolent? Here, again, the union between Jesus and God is essential.

Since Jesus was actually God in human form, then anything he did, God did. That means that God, in some sense, suffered and died on a Roman cross. What does this have to do with the evil and suffering in the world we witness today? Since we know that God took on human form—that he came down to our level, so to speak—and suffered, then we know that any suffering he allows is not due to a lack of empathy or lack of understanding. Since God was on that cross in the person of Jesus, then he personally has experienced suffering in the same manner as we do, which means we can never say that God allows suffering because he simply doesn't understand what we're going through or because he is too far removed from us. The resurrection proves, beyond a shadow of a doubt, that God "gets it." But that's not all it proves.

Not only do we know that Jesus suffered, but we can also know that he suffered for our sake. Jesus tells his followers that as the good shepherd, he "lays down his life for the sheep."[58] He's referring to us. So not only does God understand the pain and suffering that we endure; he understands it because he endured it for our sake. Many other places in the Bible affirm the same reasoning for Jesus's death. It is for *us* that he laid down his life. As an omnipotent, transcendent creator, he does not owe his creation anything. The only reason he would take on human form and go through what he went through is because he loves us and wants to secure for us a future and a hope. If God serves us in any way—if he relates to us in any way in a benevolent, gracious manner—then we know it is only because he willfully chooses to and because it is in his nature to do so.

When we look at Jesus and see God suffering for the sake of humankind, we are only left with one conclusion: God not only suffered as we suffer, but he suffered for our sakes. He suffered for us because he loves us. That means that whatever the reason God allows evil and suffering in the world, we can be certain it is *not* because he doesn't empathize, and it is *not* because he doesn't love us. Jesus's resurrection proves that God knows our suffering and endured the same suffering out of love for us.

On this side of eternity, we may never know why God allows any act of evil or instance of suffering, but we can know that it is only ever allowed from a nature that hates the evil committed and that deeply loves those who suffer. Even when we cannot understand the mind of God, we can still trust his heart. And the resurrection of Jesus is the objective evidence that allows us to do just that.

If we are ever wrestling with an issue pertaining to the nature and character of God, the resurrection shows us that we can look to Jesus for the answer. It is sometimes difficult to understand the heart of God and the way he works in the world and in our lives, but we always have a tangible expression of his full self in the person of Jesus.

Some objections to the Christian worldview, however, have less to do with the object of the worldview—the Christian understanding of God—and much more to do with those who subscribe to the worldview: Christians.

Aren't Christians hypocritical? Haven't they been the source of much injustice and oppression in the past?

Many have expressed opposition to the Christian worldview because of the demeanor and actions of Christians, both in the present and throughout the church's history. To be sure, Christians, or at least those who have identified as such, have often been guilty of hypocrisy, injustice, and self-centered oppression of others. This is a fact that is both undeniable and unfortunate. It is also a fact, though, that no true Christian should feel the need to outright deny. The entire Christian worldview is predicated on the belief that on our own, we will constantly let both ourselves and the rest of the world down. The fact that Christianity assumes the need for grace and forgiveness implies that we, as creatures, will do things that require grace and forgiveness. Christian teaching

> *Christian teaching nowhere claims to produce morally perfect people; it assumes that we are all morally broken and simply points us to the source of forgiveness and restoration.*

nowhere claims to produce morally perfect people; it assumes that we are all morally broken and simply points us to the source of forgiveness and restoration.

While this depiction of Christians as unjust or oppressive is, sadly, accurate at times, it is also woefully incomplete. Christian organizations and groups have often been the champions of equality, justice, and serving the marginalized. Martin Luther King Jr., Jesuit missionaries, and the Salvation Army are all obvious examples of this. The historical development of Christian benevolence is a separate matter, but it's important to hold on to the truth that all types of social, political, and religious identifications will have within them those who pursue things worthy of both affirmation and condemnation.

The relevant point to consider in our present discussion is simple: the past, present, and future behavior of Christian individuals and institutions have no effect on whether or not Jesus, a real person from Nazareth, rose from the dead. What someone does today or tomorrow has no effect on whether or not a historical event actually happened. That may seem dismissive, but as we noted in the opening chapter of this book, we must be careful not to conflate a concrete, objective claim with its outworking, whether said outworking is good or bad.

For instance, let's revisit our gravity analogy. Imagine our friend from earlier, the one who believes he can deny gravity, also convinces many others that they can do the same. He and all of his followers then jump off of a bridge together in an effort to demonstrate their abilities to the world. News of the tragedy goes viral. In the aftermath of the event, many individuals begin to suggest that since gravity ultimately caused them to fall to their end, it's too dangerous to teach about gravity. The reasonable people, however, insist on the very opposite. It is precisely *because* gravity's universal nature is true that we must separate it from other people's beliefs. It wasn't gravity that caused the tragedy; it was their misunderstanding of it. And their misunderstanding and the behavior that it led to have no effect on the actual nature of gravitational force. This is how we must consider the objective truthfulness of the Christian worldview. To say that Christianity isn't true because some have misunderstood and misapplied it is to say that anything that anyone has ever misunderstood or misapplied must also not be true. The validity of the Christian worldview centers on its founder, not on those who claim some version of it for themselves.

Again, as we concluded in the previous question regarding God's nature, Jesus provides for us a means of approaching any question or concern we may have pertaining to Christians and the church. If we are ever faced with a topic that piques our curiosity, brings about uncertainty, or even incites frustration, we know precisely where we ought to turn: to the one who defeated death itself.

3. If Jesus rose from the dead, any religion other than Christianity or any worldview incompatible with Christianity, by definition, cannot be true.

In an increasingly postmodern world, this point may actually garner more objection than matters of apologetics such as the problem of evil. In today's social climate, to say that someone's religion or worldview is wrong is seen as demeaning and degrading. Of course, there *are* demeaning and degrading ways to disagree with someone, but, as we discussed in Chapter 1, disagreeing in and of itself is not inherently an affront to someone's personhood and character. In fact, like we said, tolerance is not the valuing of every belief and opinion, but the valuing of every person, regardless of their beliefs and opinions. By definition, tolerance requires tolerating, which means there's something to tolerate—something you don't agree with. All of that is to say that it's crucial to distinguish between saying "your belief isn't true" and "you are not valuable."

With that, we can confidently say that the resurrection directly means that any religion other than Christianity or any worldview incompatible with Christianity cannot be true. By Christianity, I do not mean the culture and practices that are commonly associated with Christianity. It has nothing to do with Western values or conservative politics or anything of the sort. By Christianity, I mean the central, foundational claims of the Christian worldview. If Jesus came back from the dead, then he validated all of his claims of identity and purpose, and any religion or worldview that denies those claims is, by definition, incorrect. For instance, if someone's worldview suggests that Jesus was a great moral example but not divine, that worldview would be in direct opposition to what the resurrection objectively proved.

Again, this is not a matter of devaluing those who hold beliefs incompatible with the Christian worldview; it's a matter of the rules of logic. Two events that cannot occur simultaneously are said to be mutually exclusive. The same is true for two pieces of information. If fact A being true necessarily means that fact B cannot be true, then facts A and B cannot be true at the same time. If we say that the Christian worldview is fact A and a religion that denies the central tenets of Christianity is fact B, then A and B cannot both be true. If Jesus rose from the dead, then the Christian worldview—the only worldview that upholds the divinity and authority of Jesus—has an exclusive claim on factual truthfulness.

4. If Jesus rose from the dead, then he has a rightful claim to authority over the whole world.

In the timeless film *Monty Python and the Holy Grail*, King Arthur is "riding" around the countryside, searching for knights to join his quest for the Holy Grail. He stumbles upon some peasants working in the field. He addresses one, Dennis, in a less-than-polite manner. This excites Dennis to question where he gets the nerve. Arthur, being king, is taken aback by this outburst of disrespect, as he sees it, and he quickly informs Dennis that as king he deserves total allegiance. The following dialogue ensues:

> Dennis: What I object to is you automatically treat me like an inferior.
>
> King Arthur: Well, I *am* king.
>
> Dennis: Oh, king, eh? Very nice. And how'd you get that, eh? By exploiting the workers. By hanging on to outdated imperialist dogma which perpetuates the economic and social differences in our society.

King Arthur: I am your king.

Woman: Well, I didn't vote for you.

King Arthur: You don't vote for kings.

Woman: Well, how'd you become king then?

King Arthur: The Lady of the Lake, her arm clad in the purest shimmering samite held aloft Excalibur from the bosom of the water, signifying by divine providence that I, Arthur, was to carry Excalibur. That is why I am your king.

Dennis: Listen, strange women lyin' in ponds distributin' swords is no basis for a system of government. Supreme executive power derives from a mandate from the masses, not from some farcical aquatic ceremony.[59]

Aside from the classic humor, what's poignant about this exchange is that it highlights the sentiment that most of us have regarding the notion of authority. We are naturally predisposed to push back against unfounded claims of authority, particularly if we sense that authority is being or will be abused. That is why democracies, with all their headaches, are still seen as preferable to monarchies and dictatorships.

One of the most common reasons for rejecting the resurrection of Jesus, whether stated or not, is the implication that if Jesus is divine—if he is, in fact, God himself—then he has a rightful claim to authority over the whole Earth and all who inhabit it. If he is the creator in the flesh, then he obviously can justly claim authority over his creation, which includes us as created beings.

And it's not only a matter of a rightful *claim* to authority over all; in his resurrection, he actually *proves* he has authority over all by having authority over death itself. No matter our credentials, our influence, or our abilities, death comes for us all. Until Jesus, no one could ever rightfully claim authority over everything, because death remained as the final frontier, so to speak. Even the paragons of power and influence throughout history—Alexander the Great, Queen Elizabeth I, and even Genghis Khan, who at one point controlled nearly a fifth of the globe's total area—didn't have authority over death. They could command entire countries to fight for them, and yet none of them could say, "I have authority over all." Jesus is the only person who ever lived that proved that nothing—not even the great enemy, death itself—has control over him, which means he's the only person to ever live that has earned the right to be followed no matter what. At the end of Matthew's Gospel, Jesus makes this claim of authority:

> Now the eleven disciples went to Galilee, to the mountain to which Jesus had directed them. . . . And Jesus came and said to them, **"All authority in heaven and on earth has been given to me"** (emphasis added). [60]

This was after Jesus's resurrection. Imagine, though, if he had made this claim prior to his crucifixion. It would have sounded absurd. Sure, that's a claim that anyone can make. You and I could attempt to claim total authority over everything, but eventually death will call us on the carpet and show us to be either lying or delusional. But when Jesus makes this claim after rising from the dead, there's no way to argue with him. He showed that even death is subject to his will. But here is our problem. We have a difficult time accepting that Jesus's claim of having "all authority in heaven and on earth" applies to us. But if Jesus really did rise from the dead, then he has a rightful and fair claim of authority over you and over me.

This implication of Jesus's authority and his other claims can be difficult to accept. They are, after all, remarkable claims. And not only that, they could potentially require a significant shift in our worldview and lifestyle, if they are true. But again, the implications of an event have no bearing on whether the event actually occurred. The implications of the resurrection are essential to consider, but they cannot be the only starting point of our consideration. By definition, the very term *implication* assumes they are only true *if* the original premise is true. Whether or not the event occurred must be our starting point, and the implications can then be considered thereafter.

A New Approach

It is tempting to approach the truthfulness of Christianity through the lens of the implications of Christianity—to say, in other words, "I'm not able to accept this particular implication or these implications; therefore, I cannot accept the premise as true." It allows a philosophical objection to be laid over the objective, historical data. As you can see in the diagram below, this approach takes evidence for the resurrection and runs it through our objection(s), leading to the conclusion that the resurrection must not have occurred.

The problem with this approach is that it does not treat evidence as evidence. Evidence is either intrinsically sufficient to supply a conclusion or it is not. It isn't subject to desires, motives, feelings, or the like. If a detective was required to investigate a crime in which his best friend was the lead suspect, he would be expected to investigate it independent of his desire for his friend to be innocent. He would be expected to set any personal feelings aside and examine the case objectively. If he allowed his desire for his friend to be innocent to distort his analysis of the facts, we would say he approached the case incorrectly—that he did his job poorly.

When investigating the resurrection, we cannot allow any ulterior motives or objections to distort our analysis of the facts. We must allow the evidence to speak for itself. Then, as the diagram below illustrates, through the lens of the conclusion that we draw, we can work out a new approach to whatever our objection may be. We let the evidence speak for itself, and then we reevaluate the objection.

We saw this approach employed previously when we addressed the problem of evil. Rather than think to ourselves, "The evidence is convincing, but since there is evil in the world, Christianity must be false," we ought to instead think, "The evidence is convincing, and therefore Christianity must be true, which means there must be an explanation for the evil in the world that is compatible with that truth." Of course, this same approach can be applied to any other objection or problem with the Christian worldview. Whatever the hurdle, the objective evidence is enough to carry us over it, and we can then revisit and analyze the hurdle from the other side.

Asking the Real Question

I stated previously that it is essential to ask the question beneath the question. That is, we must not only ask, "What do I believe?" but we also need to ask, "*Why* do I believe what I believe?" I'd actually like to pose an additional question—the question beneath the question beneath the question, if you will. While the question of why we believe what we believe is crucial, it fundamentally stands on another question: "What do I *want* to believe?" I do not mean to unsay what I've argued previously. To be sure, *wanting* something to be true or not does not actually change whether or not it is true. It can, however, very much determine whether or not we *accept it* as truth. Specifically, this means that in addition to asking "Do I believe Jesus

> *Wanting something to be true does not actually change whether or not it is true. It can, however, very much determine whether or not we accept it as truth.*

rose from the dead?" and even in addition asking "Why do I believe or not believe that Jesus rose from the dead?" we must also ask, "Do I *want* Jesus to have risen from the dead?" For what our heart wants to believe will inevitably influence what our head decides to believe. It's the role of the head to recognize truth; it's the role of the heart to actually accept it. If our head refuses to recognize something as true, perhaps on some level it's due to our heart's unwillingness to accept what that truth could mean for us.

In one of his parables—the story of the rich man and Lazarus—Jesus highlights this relationship between the head and the heart. The rich man asks for his brothers to be warned of the fate that befell him due to his rejection of God. He asks for Lazarus, who is already dead, to be sent to his brothers, assuming that "if someone goes to them from the dead"[61] to warn them, they'll have to believe. It's difficult to disagree with him, is it not? If we encountered someone who rose from the dead, surely, we'd believe whatever he told us. But Jesus ends the parable by saying that's not necessarily the case. The rich man is told that if his brothers are not willing to let the truth transform their hearts, it will never be able to convince their heads. In other words, it's not a lack of proof that will prevent them from believing in the divinity of Jesus, but rather an unwillingness to accept the proof.

What Jesus knows and is alluding to is that there will be those who actually see him first-hand after his

If the evidence seems unconvincing, is it because it's actually unconvincing or is it because we do not want to be convinced?

resurrection and still refuse to accept it; that is, accept all that his resurrection means. Their heads will recognize the fact that he came back from the dead, but their hearts won't be ready to accept him as a divine authority. They will see that Jesus has risen from the dead, but on some level, they won't want that to be the case. We, of course, must ask if the same is true for us. If the evidence seems unconvincing, is it because it's actually unconvincing or is it because we do not want to be convinced?

Good News

Thomas Cranmer, leader of the English Reformation, taught that what the heart loves, the will chooses and the mind justifies.[62] In other words, our hearts are really in charge. As much as we would like to believe that our minds decide what we want to believe and that we conform our heart's affections to those beliefs, it is, in fact, most often the other way around. Whatever our hearts need us to choose and justify will be what we shape our lives around. That means, for the sake of the subject matter at hand, we have to first *want* to accept the implications of Jesus's resurrection before we'll be convinced of its historical truthfulness on an intellectual level. Our hearts must accept the resurrection before our minds can follow suit.

The final question is, then, "Why should we *want* Jesus to have resurrected?" In other words, "Why is Jesus's defeat over death worthy of our hearts' affections, not simply a cognitive admission?" When we really understand what the resurrection means for this world—what it means for you and for me—we'll hardly see it as a tough pill to swallow.

Indeed, there are some implications of Jesus's rising from the dead that at first can be difficult to reconcile. However, there is a reason the New Testament writers refer to what Jesus accomplished as the *gospel*, which comes from the Greek word for *good news*. Jesus's triumph over the grave is not ammunition to win religious debates; it's news—*good news*—for all who would hear and respond to it. And the implications of that news, when fully grasped, will lead us from seeing Christianity as one religion among many to seeing it as remarkable, life-changing, world-altering news that we cannot help but want to be true.

Chapter 10
A Living Hope

Our Lord has written the promise of the resurrection. Not in books alone, but in every leaf of springtime.

—Martin Luther

It wasn't until AD 451 that the Chalcedonian Creed defined and summarized the union between Jesus's human and divine natures. The Nicene Creed, which laid out the church's official beliefs regarding the Trinity, wasn't developed until AD 325. Christianity was in its second millennium before Anselm articulated what is now a predominant theory of the atonement. And there are even several key tenets of Christian orthodoxy that were not robustly communicated until after the 16th century. But while it took a combination of ecumenical councils and centuries of diverse scholarship to codify official beliefs about the meaning of Jesus's death, the nature of the Trinity, and several other important doctrines, one central belief—the news of a risen Jesus—was there from the beginning. And that news spread like wildfire throughout the Roman Empire and beyond.

Certainly, such an event is noteworthy in and of itself. But it wasn't that the event simply happened that caused the logic-defying explosion of Christianity across the ancient world; it was what the event meant—what it signified—that caused such a stir. The early Christians, not least the authors of the New Testament, believed that Jesus's resurrection did something. Because Jesus had come back from the dead, something else—something important—had happened. The apostle Peter says it this way in one of his letters:

> *According to his great mercy, he has caused us to be born again to a living hope* **through the resurrection of Jesus Christ from the dead**, *to an inheritance that is imperishable, undefiled, and unfading* (emphasis added).[63]

Peter tells his readers that God has "caused" something to happen in the world, and he has done so "through the resurrection of Jesus Christ from the dead." Specifically, he has given the world "a living hope," which Peter likens to an inheritance—one that cannot be shaken or stolen. We have several times alluded to this living hope that the early Christians held on to (and that many Christians around the world hold on to today), but what is it exactly? What is this inheritance—this future—that Jesus alone could offer and that was worth following him for, whatever the cost? And what did it have to do with Jesus's coming back from the dead? The answer lies in a peculiar word used a handful of times in the New Testament: *firstfruits*.

The Coming Harvest

In an agrarian culture, one's livelihood is determined by the firstfruits of the harvest—the first produce of a particular season. For each harvest season, there is a portion of the crop

A Living Hope

that ripens before the rest, and based on the timing and health of that first crop, you know how the rest of the harvest will turn out. If the firstfruits are healthy and ready at the right time (or if they ripen late and appear small and sickly), you know that will be the case for the rest of the crops. Whatever was true for the firstfruits will be true for everything else.

Paul uses this imagery when telling about the future hope that awaits Christians, saying that Jesus is "the firstfruits of those who have fallen asleep."[64] His readers would have understood not only exactly what that meant but also how incredible such a claim was. What Paul is saying is that because Jesus has exercised his authority over death in his own resurrection, he has proved that he can—and will—likewise exercise that same authority for anyone who trusts him to do so. In other words, what makes Jesus's resurrection so significant is not simply that he beat death, but that through him, we too can beat it. Death wasn't defeated once (however remarkable that would be); it was defeated once and for all. And because whatever is true for the firstfruits will be true for the rest of the harvest, our victory over death, which Jesus offers, will look just like his. And therein lies the unique and remarkable offer of Christianity—the offer that makes the Christian worldview worth wanting to be true.

> *Death wasn't defeated once (however remarkable that would be); it was defeated once and for all.*

A spirit hath not flesh and bones

Ask just about anyone what the hope and future of a Christian is—and you'll likely get an answer centered on going to heaven when you die. Essentially, the thought is that we all have to endure some period of time here in the physical world, and afterward we will be transported to a heavenly realm, presumably one with streets of gold winding through the clouds inhabited by floating spirits (playing harps, of course).

But while such images of heaven can be found in pagan mythology and medieval folklore (and likely in our favorite cartoons and comics), one place you might be surprised not to find them is in the Bible. In fact, the biblical authors seem to go out of their way to paint an altogether different picture. That doesn't mean a Christian isn't promised to be welcomed into God's presence when he or she dies; even Jesus affirmed that. He said to one of the criminals being crucified next to him, just moments before his death, "Today, you will be with me in Paradise."[65] That is a great hope, indeed! But it isn't the fullest picture of the hope—the living hope—that Jesus gives. There is great comfort in having assurance about life after death, but the final Christian hope lies beyond that in what New Testament scholar N. T. Wright has cleverly called "life after life after death."[66] Because while Jesus did, in spirit, welcome that criminal into God's presence on that first Good Friday, he then walked out of the tomb on that first Easter Sunday. And, as the New Testament authors are abundantly clear, he did so not *in spirit* but *in the flesh*. Here is Luke's account of one of Jesus's appearances to his disciples after his resurrection:

> *But they were startled and frightened and thought they saw a spirit. And he said to them, "Why are you troubled, and why do doubts arise in your hearts? See my hands and my feet, that it is I myself. Touch me, and see. For a spirit does not have flesh and bones as you see that I have." And when he had said this, he showed them his hands and his feet. And while they still disbelieved for joy and were marveling, he said to them, "Have you anything here to eat?" They gave him a piece of broiled fish, and he took it and ate before them.*[67]

Like many of us, the disciples did not have a framework for an encounter with a bodily resurrected person. They immediately (and understandably) assumed that they were seeing a spirit. Jesus, sympathetic to their fear and confusion, invited them to not only see the physical wounds in his hands and feet but to physically touch him. Filled with marvel and joy, the disciples still (and again, understandably) remained incredulous. And so Jesus, wanting to leave no doubt, asked for something to eat and "he took it and ate before them."

What Luke and the other Gospel writers are committed to is dispelling the possibility of the Easter message being relegated to a feel-good story. Even in the ancient world, they anticipated the assumption that Jesus's so-called resurrection was really just the carrying on of his spirit and influence—that even though he died, he now lives on, so to speak, through his teachings and his followers. That is how many view the Easter story even today. But in the accounts of Jesus's encounters with his disciples after his resurrection, we have overly clear language that Jesus came back from the dead, not in essence but in actuality. He had actual arms that hugged, teeth that chewed, and vocal cords that spoke. So yes, the Easter message reflects a lot of wonderful sentiments about the new coming from the old and spring coming after life's winters, but it is first and foremost the story of a real man who walked out of a tomb on real feet that kicked up real dust on his way to a real meal where he ate real food in the presence of his friends and family.

Again, this is what makes Paul's claim about Jesus being the firstfruits of those who have died so incredible. Whatever is true of the firstfruits is true for the rest of the harvest, right? That means that the ultimate future Jesus promises his followers is not a disembodied existence in a spaceless, timeless heaven, but instead a resurrected body—a body that is able to walk, eat, speak, hug, dance, and laugh!

We so often think of heaven as just a final escape of life's troubles that we fail to stop and wonder about life's delights. Indeed, just as Jesus promised the criminal on the cross, the Christian's death is an escape from pain and suffering into God's comfort and peace. But the future that Jesus offers is not merely an opportunity to be in the absence of ailments but to actually be in the presence of beauty and pleasure. It's not just leaving behind the old body; it's one day being raised with a new one! That's why Paul said this in his letter to the Philippians:

> *We await a Savior, the Lord Jesus Christ, who will transform our lowly body to be like his glorious body, by the power that enables him even to subject all things to himself.* [68]

Think about some of the most memorable and enjoyable

moments of your life. Would those be the same if you had no physical senses? You needed taste buds to experience those incredible meals. You needed eardrums to listen to that unforgettable concert. You needed the rods and cones in your eyes to behold the sun setting behind that mountain range. Without a physical body, the gifts of this life could never be experienced. With the risen Jesus as our firstfruits, we know that God wants to give us for all eternity those same gifts—the gifts we so greatly treasure in this life.

Of course, if we're going to have feet to walk with, that means we'll need a ground on which to walk. If we're going to have taste buds and retinas, that means we'll need meals to eat and beauty at which to marvel. And that brings us to the next reason that Jesus as our firstfruits is such spectacular news—news worth wanting. Because what the Easter story also tells us is that what God has done for Jesus he will one day do for the entire world. That is, Jesus isn't simply the firstfruits for us as people; he's also the firstfruits of God's work on a cosmic level.

The new heavens and the new earth

The opening words of the Bible read, "In the beginning, God created the heavens and the earth."[69] The words that follow go on to tell of God's ordering of the universe and all that is within it. Trees and mountains and rivers and birds and stars and elephants—they're all painted onto God's canvas of creation. But as it currently stands, that creation is transient. Stars die and form supernovas; animals die and decompose into organic material.

One day, though, that will no longer be the case. Just as the biblical narrative opens with the creation of the heavens and the Earth, it closes with the creation of the *new* heavens and the *new* Earth. The apostle John, the author of Revelation, wrote:

> *Then I saw a new heaven and a new earth, for the first heaven and the first earth had passed away. . . . And I saw the holy city, new Jerusalem, coming down out of heaven from God. . . . And I heard a loud voice from the throne saying, "Behold, the dwelling place of God is with man. He will dwell with them, and they will be his people, and God himself will be with them as their God. . . . He will wipe away every tear from their eyes, and death shall be no more, neither shall there be mourning, nor crying, nor pain anymore, for the former things have passed away.*[70]

In an intentional echo of those first words in Genesis, John is saying that just as all things in life pass away, in some sense, so too will the Earth itself. But just as Jesus has been resurrected, so will the Earth. And as God is reunited with his creation, things will be made as they are meant to be. Pain and sorrow are left behind—no death, no mourning, no crying—and the goodness and beauty of God's creation will be fully restored. And again, what is true of the firstfruits is true for the rest of the harvest, so just as Jesus maintained his physical composition, so too will the new Earth. Think about that. That means real grass for us to roll in, real wine to drink, and real instruments to play. It means real paint to brush across a canvas, real coffee beans to roast, and real stars to gaze at.

It saddens me that I've often heard people express genuine worry that they will be bored in heaven. Such worries can only be birthed out of a radical misunderstanding of what eternity with our creator will be like. Of course, if our future hope was to exist as a disembodied member of an eternal choir in the clouds, I could sympathize. But the future that we're promised on the new Earth is nothing like that, and thus, it will be anything but boring. In fact, it's precisely the opposite. It's the fulfillment of everything we were created to desire and enjoy. It's no wonder, then, that the descriptions of the Christian hope are unashamedly presented as invitations to enjoy God and his gifts forever.

Accepting the Offer

On June 8, 1941, C. S. Lewis preached a sermon at the Church of St. Mary the Virgin in Oxford, England, that shaped the landscape of Christian thought in more ways than he could have anticipated. The opening premise of that sermon, which he called "The Weight of Glory," is among the most influential teachings in my life and no doubt in the lives of many others:

> The New Testament has lots to say about self-denial, but not about self-denial as an end in itself. We are told to deny ourselves and to take up our crosses in order that we may follow Christ; and nearly every description of what we shall ultimately find if we do so contains an *appeal to desire*. If there lurks in most modern minds the notion that to desire our own good and earnestly to hope for the *enjoyment* of it is a bad thing, I submit that this notion has crept in from Kant and the Stoics and is no part of the Christian faith. Indeed, if we consider the *unblushing promises of reward and the staggering nature of the rewards*

promised in the Gospels, it would seem that Our Lord finds our desires, not too strong, but too weak. We are half-hearted creatures, fooling about with drink and sex and ambition when *infinite joy* is offered us, like an ignorant child who wants to go on making mud pies in a slum because he cannot imagine what is meant by the offer of a holiday at the sea. We are far too easily pleased (emphasis added).[71]

Notice the language Lewis uses to describe the future hope of the Christian: "an appeal to desire," "enjoyment," "unblushing . . . and staggering nature of the rewards promised," and "infinite joy." He argues that the idea that following Jesus is ultimately about denying oneself pleasure and enjoyment is an utter misunderstanding of what the New Testament communicates. To the contrary, recognizing Jesus as Lord and entrusting him with your life is, in actuality, like trading in "mud pies in a slum" for "a holiday at the sea."

And this brings us back full circle to our opening illustration: the news of a distant relative leaving a fortune in your name. Again, it's not something you blindly accept, but it's also certainly not something you dismiss without careful investigation. If the offer isn't genuine—if it's a scam—then you've nothing to lose. But if it is genuine—if your investigation of its validity led you to believe the news is legitimate—then you'd accept the offer in a heartbeat.

My hope is that this book has helped answer the important questions in that investigative effort. I hope I have answered why Jesus's resurrection is the most significant event in our world's history. I hope I have shown that such an event—

this supernatural occurrence—is both philosophically and scientifically possible. I hope I have successfully made a case for why Jesus's resurrection is the only logical conclusion we can draw from an abundance of historical evidence. More than that—more than arguing why Jesus's resurrection is something we can and should believe to be true—I hope I have shown why a full understanding of what the resurrection means for you, for me, and for the world we live in makes it something we should *want* to be true. I hope this book has helped eliminate the uncertainty surrounding the questions "Is the offer legitimate?" and "Is it worth wanting?" and leaves only the question "Will I accept it?"

Answering the door

In Revelation, the last book of the Bible, the risen Jesus says:

> *I stand at the door and knock. If anyone hears my voice and opens the door, I will come in . . . and eat with him.*[72]

I don't know what your experience with Jesus has been in the past. Perhaps you consider yourself a spiritual person seeking answers wherever you can; maybe you are hardened to the idea of any sort of religion altogether; or maybe you have been a Christian for as long as you can remember. Whatever the case, my appeal to you is this: please do not view Jesus as the founder of a religion. Do not think of him as simply another moral teacher or yet another revolutionary. In a sense, he is those things (and more). But he is primarily the only person to ever conquer death and the only person who can legitimately offer that same hope to you and to me. And that is something that he is eager to do. He now stands at the door and knocks, desiring to be welcomed into our lives and give us the victory he has achieved. All we must do is answer the door and let him in.

What does answering the door look like? Paul tells us in his letter to the church in Rome:

> *If you confess with your mouth that Jesus is Lord and believe in your heart that God raised him from the dead, you will be saved.* [73]

Believe in his resurrection and confess him as Lord. And what Paul understood was that those two things are really two sides to the same coin. He knows that genuinely believing that Jesus has been raised from the dead will lead us to acknowledge him as Lord. And while that term *Lord* may at first sound hyper-spiritual or churchy, it would have had a concrete, pointed meaning to Paul's original audience.

Everyone in Rome knew that Caesar was lord. Quite literally, he ruled the known world. Everyone owed allegiance to him and him alone. So when Paul makes the claim that Jesus, not Caesar, is Lord and that he has proved his rightful ascension to the world's throne by coming back from the dead, he is telling his readers that there is a new king—a new Caesar, so to speak—who is worthy of their allegiance. It may have been a radical claim (and one that would cost many of them everything they had), but when confronted with the reality of the resurrection, it was a claim they could not refute.

Because Jesus's resurrection vindicates him as the rightful King of God's coming Kingdom—because it rightly gives him authority over all things—the invitation into that

A Living Hope

Kingdom only requires of us one thing: recognize him as that rightful King—as Lord. Just as the average Roman citizen understood the need for Caesar's provision and protection, we must likewise recognize our need for the provision and protection that Jesus alone can give. We must acknowledge that he alone can protect us from the sting of death and that he alone can give us all the things we were designed and created to enjoy. The difference between Caesar and Jesus, though, is that Caesar's kingdom eventually came to an end, but Jesus's Kingdom never will. That provision and protection that Jesus offers—that he's eager to give—is ours to enjoy forever.

What does answering the door and letting Jesus in look like? It's the simple recognition that without him you have no hope—no hope of escaping death and no hope of enjoying the presence of God forever, which, as the Psalmist tells us, is where the "fullness of joy" and "pleasures forevermore" are found. [74]

Friends, when we come to the tomb of Jesus, we won't find a body. What we'll find is an offer—an offer to one day wake up from the sleep of death, an offer to cultivate and experience an imperishable new home, an offer to sing and dance and eat and hug and laugh with loved ones, all in the presence of God for all eternity. That's the hope—the living hope—that the empty tomb gives to us. All we have to do is receive it.

Conclusion

I gave in and admitted that God was God.
—C. S. Lewis

If at the very least this book has helped catalyze a journey of questioning and discovery regarding your worldview, I'm grateful for that. In the end, none of us can remain blissfully uncertain on matters of our world's origin, the human condition, and, most notably, the afterlife. They are topics worthy of attention, and it is my hope that if your questions weren't answered here, you won't be satisfied until they are elsewhere.

If, however, this book has done something more—if it has convinced or at least begun to convince you that Jesus wasn't merely a good moral example who passed on a few helpful teachings, then perhaps you are wondering: *What now?*

What does accepting the truth of Jesus's resurrection and its implications mean for my life? What does it mean to acknowledge him as Lord and give him my allegiance? These questions can easily become overwhelming because there are numerous depictions and versions of Christianity presented to us from all sides. And it's likely that they are accompanied by their fair share of connotations, many of which are confusing or negative—or both. I can empathize. Even as someone who is utterly convinced of Jesus's divinity, I seem to have more questions than answers most days, and I believe that any honest Christian will admit the same. While believing in Jesus does give us an unshakable hope, it doesn't magically clean up everything in our lives or tie up all the loose ends of our doubts and questions. So I'd like to offer some final words of encouragement as you begin to live out what I can confidently say will be the most important decision of your life.

First, it's important to dispel any preconceived notions you may have of what it means to be a Christian—not because all of them are necessarily inaccurate, but because it's essential that you learn on your own which ones are accurate and which ones are not. Most importantly, though, I implore you to abandon any belief that Christianity can be equated with a list of dos and don'ts. The message of Jesus is anything *but* another religious system to be followed. In fact, it was the religious leaders of Jesus's day that wanted Jesus dead and turned him over to the Romans to be crucified. That's another matter for another book, but the fact remains that it is possible for someone to be very religious and nevertheless want nothing to do with Jesus.

What *does* it mean, then, to acknowledge who he is and what he accomplished on our behalf? Jesus gives us the answer in the words that began and framed his entire public ministry:

Repent and believe in the gospel.[75]

Admittedly, words like "repent" can conjure up less-than-pleasant images of hellfire and brimstone preaching, but that is not what Jesus is talking about here. We'll get to what he does mean shortly, but first I'd like to address what he means by *believe in the gospel*.

As we've previously seen, the word *gospel* comes from the Greek word that means *good news* or *good message*. Jesus begins his ministry with a proclamation of the good news about what God is doing in the world—specifically, what God is doing *through him*. He's saying, "God is on a mission in this world, and he's accomplishing that mission through me." We explored what the ultimate goal of that mission is in Chapter 10—the reuniting of God and his people on a new Earth—and we discussed how Jesus's resurrection serves to foreshadow what the completion of that mission will look like. What we have yet to answer, though, is how the accomplishments of Jesus—not only his resurrection, but also his life and, particularly, his death—accomplish that mission and secure for us the hope that we're offered. This is something that's essential to consider, because even the most wonderful picture of the future isn't *good news* if there's no way for us to attain it. The gospel, then, is not only the news of what lies ahead, but also the news of how God gets us there.

Bad News, Good News

The first step in understanding the good news of what God is doing in the world is coming to grips with the fact that there must be, by necessity, bad news. The joy of being rescued is only truly known when there is something from which we need to be rescued. The presence of a solution necessitates the presence of a problem. What is the problem with the world, then? It's that we have turned from God—from the one who designed and created the world and us who inhabit it. We have rejected his leadership in favor of our own. This rejection is what the Bible calls sin. Again, I understand the connotations this word may carry with it, and, again, I ask that you set them aside. Sin is not merely, as many portray it to be, the breaking of arbitrary rules. It's deeper than that. It's the heart-posture that says to God, in the words of William Henley's "Invictus," "I am the master of my fate; I am the captain of my soul." It's the desire that we all share to be in control of our own lives—to belong to oneself and no one else.

This commitment to autonomy—this worship of self over and against the worship of God—is what is ultimately wrong with the world and what must be set right if we are to enjoy God and his gifts as we were created to do. And that is precisely what the accomplishments of Jesus were aimed at. It is through him—through his life, death, and resurrection—that our sin is overcome and we are put right with God once more—not simply in the sense of being forgiven for this and that bad thing that we did, but in that we are actually reconciled to him in a way that undoes our rejection of him and all its damaging effects, both to our own lives and to the world. When Jesus said on the cross, "It is finished," [76] that is what he is referring to. He is claiming that he has tangibly accomplished a way for us to have the relationship with our creator that we were intended to have and that the world can be made right into what it was intended to be. That's what Jesus is proclaiming as good news. That's what he's asking us to "believe in."

This brings us back to the term we tabled for the moment: *repent*. Only when we understand (1) the problem with the world and (2) how God is solving that problem—namely, through Jesus—can we then understand what it means to repent. Oftentimes, repentance is equated to the call to simply stop doing bad things. I think we all can agree that we'd like everyone to do fewer "bad things," but that's not primarily what Jesus means. If the problem with the world is that we've rejected the presence and rule of God and the good news is that God, through Jesus, has made a way for us back into that presence and rule, then repentance is simply the act of actually *accepting* that presence and rule back into our lives.

Me or Him?

At the heart of repentance, then, is a choice—a choice to give up control of our lives. It means to abdicate the throne of our hearts and allow Jesus to sit there, knowing he makes a far better king than we ever could be. When Jesus says, "Follow me,"[77] repentance is saying, "I will." The difficulty, of course, is that following Jesus necessarily means ceasing to follow ourselves, something that hardly comes naturally.

Here is where having assurance in Jesus's resurrection becomes so essential. Whenever we are tempted to believe that we may know better—that maybe we are, in fact, more qualified to decide what's best for us and for the world— we are reminded that between us and Jesus, only one is powerful enough to come back from the dead. And while acknowledging our own limitations may not be something we're initially excited about doing, it's actually quite freeing, and, ultimately, it's what makes following Jesus uniquely comforting. Because when everything else in the world is telling us to be good enough and to measure up, handing our lives to Jesus is the liberating admission that, quite simply, we don't have to. When we place our trust in and find our hope in *him* rather than in ourselves, it means that our inadequacy and weakness don't have the final say; his goodness and his power do.

Yes, the notion of surrendering control goes against everything in our beings, but remember that in surrendering control, we're *not* surrendering joy. Many make the mistake of thinking that in following Jesus they must be giving up a chance at happiness. Hopefully, the hope and future laid out in Chapter 10 helps dispel that notion and any of the sort. Hopefully we will come to realize that the *opposite* is true—that surrendering control is not the surrender of joy, but surrender of that which is *preventing* us from finding joy. Jesus said regarding his followers, "I came that they may have life and have it abundantly."[78] And he's the only one who has proved his ability to actually give that to us, not just in this life, but forever in the next.

"Remember Me"

Following Jesus doesn't mean you have to be perfect. It means trusting in the one who is. It doesn't mean you have to have all the answers. It means trusting in the one who does. It doesn't mean you have to have everything under control. It means trusting in the one who always will. And in case you're thinking that it's too late for you to make that decision to trust him, I invite you to recall the man being crucified next to Jesus, who, with his last breath, recognized the futility of trying to be his own savior—his own god—and asked Jesus one thing: "Remember me when you come into your kingdom."[79] And, more importantly, I invite you to recall Jesus's immediate and unconditional promise to do so.

In walking out of the tomb, Jesus says to us, "See what I am capable of. Witness the power I have over all of life's enemies, including sin and death. I've defeated them. All you must do is believe and trust that I can do the same for you." Repentance is just that—admitting that we can't defeat those enemies on our own and inviting Jesus to do so in our stead.

That's what is asked of each of us. That's all it takes: laying down our arms—surrendering our lives to the one who is owed our allegiance and who can give us what we all desire. We say to him, "Jesus, in living for myself—in following myself—I have been seeking after joy that I know only you can provide. I have been searching for hope that only you can offer. So I choose now to follow you instead and give to you my heart, my will, and my future. I ask that you remember me in your Kingdom—where I am eager to enjoy your presence and your blessings forever."

I pray that you will make that decision, if you have not already, and that you discover the joy that it most assuredly brings.

Acknowledgments

As is the case with all of life's endeavors, the number of roads that have converged to make this book possible are too many to number. The unique opportunities that I've been afforded are not lost on me, and reflecting on them is humbling. I would, however, like to express my gratitude to those who have played a direct part in this process.

I must first thank my wife, Kayla. Sweetheart, it would be nearly impossible to overstate how integral your support has been. No matter how many long nights were needed to hit deadlines, you patiently continued to encourage me. No matter how many times your requests to read it were met with my insecure response, "It's not ready yet," you remained gracious. In no uncertain terms, this book would hardly be what it is without you. Eden Grace, your mama is a special lady.

Thank you, also, to Justin. Not many people can call the same person their boss, their pastor, and their best friend. Thank you for taking a chance on me, for always encouraging me to exercise my gifts, and for not just saying you love my family, but proving it time and time again. Most importantly, in this book and in life itself, thank you for always pressing me to exercise objectivity and integrity and for never letting me get away with saying something without being able to substantiate it.

To my parents, you've made more sacrifices than I can count and then some. Mom and Jay, thank you for always fighting for my education. It remains and will remain one of the biggest graces in my life. Dad, thank you for never passing on the opportunity to build my library and for not only fueling my craving to grow in knowledge, but also for reminding me to do so for the right reasons.

Lastly, thank you to the man to whom this book is dedicated, my grandfather. Bapa, you've not only shown me the world; you've taught me how to truly appreciate it. Thank you for everything you've done and continually do for our family. Thank you for the conversations on theology, philosophy, and history that go long into the night. You've played a bigger role in this book than I can express, and I look forward to hearing your thoughts over a glass of rosé.

Additional Resources

Regardless of where you stand in your opinion about the Christian worldview, it's my hope that you will continue to explore the matters discussed in this book. To that end, I'd like to recommend only three works that I believe, if read with thoughtful intentionality, will be of tremendous benefit. It would be hard to overstate how formative these works have been in my own life and in the lives of countless others.

My guess is that, after reading *this* book, you will hardly be surprised at the names that appear below.

Happy reading.

Mere Christianity, C. S. Lewis

The Reason for God, Tim Keller

Surprised by Hope, N. T. Wright

Notes

Introduction
1. Acts 17:2; 17:4; 19:8

Chapter 1
2. John 20:6–8

Chapter 2
3. John 7:2–5
4. Richard Walzer (trans.), *Galen on Jews and Christians* (London: Oxford University Press, 1949), 16.
5. 1 Corinthians 15:19

Chapter 3
6. Richard Dawkins, *River Out of Eden: A Darwinian View of Life* (New York: Basic Books, 1995), 133.
7. *Merriam-Webster* online. Accessed June 9, 2017. https://www.merriam-webster.com/dictionary/science.
8. Charles Darwin, *On the Origin of Species* (2nd ed.) (London: Murray, 1860), 484.
9. *The Privileged Planet*. Dir. Lad Allen. Video. Illustra Media and Randolph Productions, 2004.
10. John Boslough, *Stephen Hawking's Universe*. Documentary, 1997.

11. Ker Than, "How Did Life Arise on Earth?" LiveScience, 1 September 2016. Accessed June 10, 2017. https://www.livescience.com/1804-greatest-mysteries-life-arise-earth.html.
12. *The Privileged Planet.*
13. Jerry A. Coyne, *Why Evolution Is True* (New York: Viking Penguin, 2009).
14. Michael Shermer, *Why Darwin Matters* (New York: Owl Books, 2006), 65.
15. Richard Dawkins, *The Blind Watchmaker* (New York: W.W. Norton & Company, 1996), 21.
16. Sir Fred Hoyle, "The Universe: Past and Present Reflections." *Engineering & Science*, November 1981, 12. Accessed June 10, 2017. http://calteches.library.caltech.edu/527/2/Hoyle.pdf.
17. Richard C. Lewontin, "Billions and Billions of Demons," *The New York Review of Books*, 9 January 1997. Accessed June 10, 2017 http://www.nybooks. com/articles/1997/01/09/billions-and-billions-of-demons/.

Chapter 5

18. C. S. Lewis, "Modern Theology and Biblical Criticism" (1969), BYU Studies Quarterly, Vol. 9, Issue 1, Article 5, 36. Accessed 10 June 2017. http://scholarsarchive.byu.edu/cgi/viewcontent.cgi?article=1324&context=byusq.
19. Luke 1:1–4
20. Richard A. Burridge, *Four Gospels, One Jesus?* (London: Society for Promoting Christian Knowledge, 1994), 6.

Notes

21. Ibid., 7.
22. Luke 14:26
23. John 6:53–57
24. John 6:60
25. Matthew 16:21–22; John 18:13–27
26. Mark 4:38; John 13:21–29
27. 1 Corinthians 15:3–6
28. C. S. Lewis. *God in the Dock* (Grand Rapids: William B. Eerdmans Publishing, 1970), 66–67.

Chapter 6

29. I first encountered the following attributes of the resurrection accounts and the importance of them listening to a lecture by Bishop of Durham N.T. Wright, titled "Did Jesus Really Rise from the Dead?" delivered on March 16, 2007, at Roanoke College. It can be found online at https://www.youtube.com/watch?v=KnkNKIJ_dnw and is a helpful resource in a further investigation of the early developments of these accounts.
30. The law of noncontradiction states that contradictory statements cannot both be true in the same sense and at the same time. Discrepancies between complementary accounts of a story are not contradictory statements, given that they are not stating things that cannot be true in the same sense and at the same time.
31. John 20:15
32. Luke 24:16
33. John 21:12

34. Luke 24:11
35. John 20:31

Chapter 7
36. "What Have I Done?" *Les Misérables*, 2012.
37. John 7:2–5
38. Hegesippus, Fragments from the Acts of the Church. Concerning the Martyrdom of James, the Brother of the Lord, Book V. Google Books, 143.
39. Ibid.
40. 1 Corinthians 15:3–10
41. Matthew 16:22; Mark 4:38; Matthew 26:40
42. Tertullian, *Apologeticum*. Accessed June 10, 2017. http://www.tertullian.org/works/apologeticum.html.

Chapter 8
43. W.D. Edwards, W.J. Gabel, and F.E. Hosmer, "On the Physical Death of Jesus Christ." Journal of the American Medical Association. March 21, 1986; 255:11, 1455–1463.
44. J. Warner Wallace, *Alive: A Cold-Case Approach to the Resurrection* (Colorado Springs: David C. Cook, 2014).
45. David Strauss, *The Life of Jesus for the People, Vol. 1*, 2nd Ed. (London: Williams and Norgate, 1879), 412.
46. Matthew 27:62–66
47. Wallace, 26–27.
48. John 19:38–41
49. Mark 15:47
50. Wallace.

51. Philip Schaff, *History of the Christian Church, Vol. 1: Apostolic Christianity* (Peabody, MA: Hendrickson Publishers, AD 1–100).

Chapter 9

52. Jonathan Edwards, "A Divine and Supernatural Light" (sermon: Northampton, 1734). Accessed June 10, 2017. http://www.ccel.org/e/edwards/sermons/supernatural_light.html.
53. Aldous Huxley, *Ends and Means* (New York: Harper & Brothers Publishers, 1937), 270.
54. Tim Keller, *The Reason for God* (New York: Penguin Group, 2008), 16-17.
55. John 10:30
56. Colossians 1:15, 19
57. Matthew 23:37
58. John 10:11
59. *Monty Python and the Holy Grail*. Dirs. Terry Gilliam, Terry Jones (Columbia Pictures, 1975).
60. Matthew 28:16–18
61. Luke 16:30
62. "Dr. Ashley Null on Thomas Cranmer" (Interview: ACL News at Moore College, September 2001).

Chapter 10

63. 1 Peter 1:3–4
64. 1 Corinthians 15:20
65. Luke 23:43
66. N.T. Wright, *Surprised by Hope* (New York: HarperCollins, 2008), 197.
67. Luke 24:37–43

68. Philippians 3:20-21
69. Genesis 1:1
70. Revelation 21:1–4
71. C. S. Lewis, *The Weight of Glory: and Other Addresses* (New York: HarperCollins, 2001), 25–26.
72. Revelation 3:20
73. Romans 10:9
74. Psalm 16:11

Conclusion
75. Mark 1:15
76. John 19:30
77. Matthew 4:19
78. John 10:10
79. Luke 23:42

www.ingramcontent.com/pod-product-compliance
Lightning Source LLC
LaVergne TN
LVHW051520070426
835507LV00023B/3216